Peaceful Leadership

Tools and Techniques for Fostering Psychological Safety, Trust, and Inclusion in Your Organization

By

Jeremy Pollack, Ph.D.

Luke Wiesner, M.S.

Sara Jeckovich, M.A.

Founders at the Peaceful Leadership Institute

PEACEFUL
Leadership Institute

For general information on our other products and services or to obtain technical support, please contact us at support@peacefuleadership.org or (305) 209-2033.

Peaceful Leadership Institute publishes its books in a variety of electronic and print formats. Some content that appears in print may not be available in electronic books, and vice versa.

ISBN: Print 979-8-218-37481-5 | eBook 979-8-218-37573-7

Contents

Introduction

Workplace conflict is ubiquitous. It occurs in every type of organization, in every industry, at all levels of power. The reason for this is quite simple: Conflict is inevitable in *any* relationship where people are at least somewhat dependent on each other to achieve their goals. The workplace, where employees must work together towards a common mission, is an intricate web of precisely these kinds of relationships. So, it's only natural that conflicts should arise.

We typically think of conflict as a negative experience— a source of discomfort and stress. But most people don't recognize that in spite of its sometimes-undesirable consequences, conflict is also critical to success. That's because conflict is hands-down the most powerful catalyst for growth, progress, and transformation. This is as true in a relationship between romantic partners as it is for coworker relationships at an organization. With every conflict comes an immense opportunity. The trick is understanding how to manage conflict effectively—how to leverage conflict creatively to advance one's relationships and the mission—

rather than mismanage conflict, which can lead to unhealthy or destructive outcomes.

Effectively addressing conflict is what the three of us have been helping organizations and employees do for more than a decade. Over the years, we've noticed the same few themes rise to the surface, regardless of the situation, company, or relationship at play. Among them, there emerged one primary indicator of long-standing, unhealthy, and destructive situations: ineffective leadership.

In more than 90% of workplace conflicts, we have found that leadership has either directly or indirectly played a role in the generation and/or maintenance of unhealthy conflicts. That is, leaders have either been directly involved in the conflict, or have contributed to a culture in which unhealthy conflicts were allowed to grow and fester. In most cases, leaders had not been properly trained, especially when it came to skills that facilitate appropriate responses to conflict.

So, when we put our heads together to figure out how we could best help our clients prevent further escalation of unhealthy conflicts, we knew we had to start with leadership. Specifically, we knew more leaders needed to be properly trained to see the opportunities in conflict, to feel comfortable navigating conflict, and to feel confident in their abilities to build and maintain cultures of peace, productivity, and innovation. Hence, the theory of Peaceful Leadership was born.

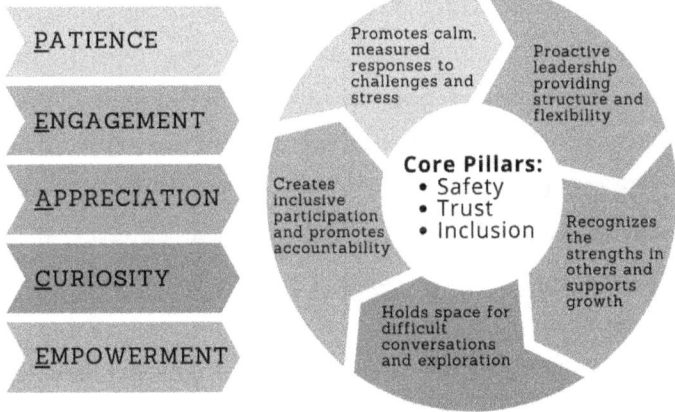

PATIENCE

ENGAGEMENT

APPRECIATION

CURIOSITY

EMPOWERMENT

Promotes calm, measured responses to challenges and stress

Proactive leadership providing structure and flexibility

Creates inclusive participation and promotes accountability

Core Pillars:
- Safety
- Trust
- Inclusion

Recognizes the strengths in others and supports growth

Holds space for difficult conversations and exploration

Peaceful Leadership is a critical skills framework designed to teach leaders how to create cultures that satisfy the core needs of their inhabitants and, therefore, help their team members truly thrive. The model of Peaceful Leadership has been used in organizations of all sizes and types and translated and applied to leaders in more than 80 industries, including government, education, and even in community and family settings.

In line with peace and conflict psychology research, the theory of Peaceful Leadership was developed with human psychological needs in mind. These needs, when unfulfilled or threatened, lead to unhealthy or destructive conflicts. When these needs are met and satisfied, however, they naturally lead to peace. That's why Peaceful Leadership centers around three psychocultural markers of a peaceful organization, which we refer to as the **Three Pillars of Peaceful Leadership**:

- Psychological Safety
- Employee Trust
- Inclusion

The Pillars are not exactly what theorists would call "basic psychological needs," as "basic" or "irreducible" needs would be even more fundamental to human thriving. Conceptually, the three Pillars can be thought of instead as *a merger between basic psychological needs and the characteristics of a culture*. When the Pillars are unstable in an organization or workplace relationship, systemic conflict is a natural result. When they are stable, the results are greater peace, productivity, innovation, and work satisfaction. All of our efforts as Peaceful Leaders will, therefore, aim to establish and stabilize these three Pillars.

To accomplish this, the Peaceful Leadership model identifies five **core competencies** that are essential for satisfying team members' psychological needs and hence solidifying the three Pillars in a team or organization. These competencies highlight the most prominent themes we have noticed in working with organizations experiencing conflict. When leaders are not competent in these areas, unhealthy conflict tends to emerge.

The five Core Competencies are:

- Patience
- Engagement
- Appreciation
- Curiosity
- Empowerment

You'll notice (conveniently) that they make up the acronym P.E.A.C.E. In this book, we will discuss best practices for several practical skills and techniques that embody these competencies and ultimately serve the three Pillars, such as:

- Regulating your own stress and emotions
- Receiving and giving feedback

- Providing strength-based growth
- Addressing difficult behaviors
- Mediating employee conflict
- Promoting accountability, and more...

When implemented properly, the skills in this book have been found to build and maintain peace at work. In Chapter 1, we will present a more in-depth overview of the Peaceful Leadership model, including a robust introduction to the three Pillars 1. Chapters 2 through 4 each provide a snapshot of one of the Pillars—psychological safety, employee trust, and inclusion—highlighting their importance and how we can cultivate them in the workplace. Then, the remaining five chapters each tackle a core competency. Within each of these chapters, we will present practical skills and techniques for carrying out the responsibilities most relevant to their respective competency.

Ultimately, our goal is to teach leaders to create environments where people can thrive. What sorts of environments do people thrive in? Environments that keep people engaged, stimulated, and growing, all while feeling valued, included, and supported. These are environments where conflicts become opportunities for growth rather than pathways to toxicity and destruction.

By the end of this book, you should feel equipped to address conflict early, navigate difficult conversations, give and receive feedback effectively, and generally lead people in a way that establishes a culture of peace and well-being. As you move through each chapter, take time to reflect on ways you can implement these tools in your organization and with your team members. You will not be perfect—none of us are. So, do your best, get creative, and hey, try to have some fun.

CHAPTER 1

Overview of the Model and Core Pillars

There are several thoroughly researched and extremely useful leadership theories and styles developed over the last century. Some of the most progressive and applicable to the modern workforce include coaching leadership, servant leadership, transformational leadership, and resonant leadership— all of which focus heavily on emotional intelligence, relationship building, and employee development.

Peaceful Leadership Theory (PLT), however, is unique in that it introduces two additional primary elements to the field of leadership. First, PLT was developed through and framed within the psychology of peace and conflict, with a specific emphasis on training leaders to create peace-oriented and conflict-resilient cultures. That is, leaders who possess the confidence and competence to navigate, manage, and resolve conflicts effectively while establishing best practices for sustaining a peaceful organizational culture. Secondly, PLT starts from a framework of basic psychological needs. As we discussed in the introduction, when combined with the characteristics of a culture, these needs create the three pillars of the Peaceful Leadership model: psychological safety, employee trust, and inclusion.

4 Psychological Needs

To survive and thrive, human beings require the fulfillment of a few basic needs. Physically, humans need food, water, temperature regulation, security, and a functional nervous system. That's obvious. But quite extraordinarily, we're also constantly looking to satisfy a set of basic psychological needs.

There have been many theories of basic psychological needs espoused over the last century, each identifying various potential needs and calling them by various names. Pulling from this philosophical and scientific literature on psychological needs, we as workplace Peacebuilders have identified four psychological needs of employees that, when undermined, consistently cause conflict:

- Respect
- Identity
- Safety
- Control

Respect refers to someone believing that they are treated fairly and equally within the framework of any particular system or culture.

Identity is a three-dimensional construct, referring to the sense of being a) competent and valuable in one's role (one's "organizational identity"), b) accepted as a member of the social groups with which one identifies (one's "social identity"), and c) valued as a human being (one's "individual identity").

Safety is a two-dimensional construct referring to a) the perception of security in one's job (i.e., security in their particular role and the security of the company as a whole) and b) the trust that one will not be humiliated or attacked by leaders or colleagues.

Control refers to the level of autonomy one has over when, where, and how one works, including the level of authority or agency one maintains in decisions that will affect one's work life.

In order to satisfy these four psychological needs, leaders and their organizations must establish particular practices and structures. Within the framework of Peaceful Leadership Theory, we have identified three psychocultural "pillars" critical to developing and maintaining a peaceful, productive culture. These Pillars directly impact the psychological needs of the individuals in the system.

The Three Pillars of Peaceful Leadership: An Overview

A Peaceful Leader understands the pressures that unhealthy or destructive conflict has on an organization. Rather than running away from conflict, intervening without the necessary skills, or just hoping that it will go away, a Peaceful Leader approaches conflict as an opportunity for growth, trust-building, learning, and innovation, as well as an opportunity to address underlying issues that may be affecting the well-being of the organization and its people. Peaceful Leaders feel equipped to do this because they have the knowledge and skills to effectively understand and address conflict. And this starts with an understanding of three primary psychocultural constructs—what we call the Three Pillars of Peaceful Leadership.

The first pillar is **psychological safety**. For our purposes, we will define psychological safety as *the degree to which an employee feels safe to speak their mind, be bold, and risk failure in order to better serve the organization*. The second pillar is **employee trust**. Although this may sound obvious, we will define trust as *the extent to which one is confident in another person's or system's intentions and abilities*. The third pillar is **inclusion**, which we shall define as *the act of considering multiple perspectives and voices, which typically creates a sense of belonging and being of value*. In the following chapters, we will unpack these pillars and offer practical tools to enhance them in your organization.

Inner Peace & Self-Leadership

In the conflict field, practitioners often highlight an important concept, which has become somewhat of a cliché: peace starts from within. In other words, one cannot build peace with others if one is not at peace within oneself. You must *be* at peace to *bring* peace. This is as true for leadership as it is for peace. In other words, one cannot lead others if one is not self-led. You must be self-led to lead others. What does it mean to be self-led? It is, perhaps, exactly as it sounds: the ability to employ the same leadership styles and approaches to yourself as you do with your team.

A self-led Peaceful Leader, therefore, creates a psychologically safe relationship with oneself. This means you allow yourself to make mistakes, take risks, fail, and explore without the risk of humiliating, shaming, or resenting yourself.

To practice trust, a Peaceful Leader exhibits consistent, predictable, self-directed thoughts and behavior. In other words, you wouldn't practice self-care in one moment and then beat yourself up the next. Rather, you would establish a consistent practice and healthy balance of self-compassion, ambition, gentleness, and drive.

A self-inclusive Peaceful leader does not shut out or repress certain emotions or intuitions because they are uncomfortable or inconvenient. Instead, you allow space for all your feelings and thoughts to arise, considering the entire spectrum that comprises YOU when making decisions and enacting life choices.

Extending the notion of self-leadership to the five core competencies of the PLT model, being a Peaceful Leader also means that you practice being patient, engaging, appreciative, curious, and empowering toward yourself.

As you embark on becoming a peaceful leader for others, take the initiative to discover where you are not practicing inner peace and self-leadership. In general, we would recommend looking into personal growth and self-discovery work, such as mindfulness, meditation, yoga, coaching or psychotherapy, nutrition counseling, and other self-care practices.

Remember, your core mission as a leader is to create an environment where people can thrive. That includes an internal environment for yourself and an external environment for others where the three pillars are established and your basic psychological needs are met.

So, what exactly does this environment look like, and what steps can be taken to create such an environment? In the next chapter, we will teach you how to establish the first pillar: psychological safety.

Introduction to the Case Narrative

In each chapter, we will present a running case narrative derived from a real client experience to illustrate what being a Peaceful Leader looks like in practice and what leadership deficiencies may lead to. As we introduce the three Pillars and five core competencies of a Peaceful Leader, we will use this narrative to analyze the Leader-Team dynamics. As you read the material, we hope it will encourage greater self-reflection and awareness. We've altered the names and other identifying information; however, the storyline and specific conflict dynamics are derived from a real workplace intervention we helped manage.

Manager & Direct Report: Connor and Renee at WDP Warehouse

It was 8:10 am, and Renee was still not at the warehouse. Her shift started at 8:00 am, and this was the fourth time in the last two weeks that she had been late. Connor, the Warehouse Manager, was getting frustrated.

Connor was a long-tenured employee with WDP Warehouse. His tenure surpassed nine years at that point, with various roles and responsibilities, starting as a Stocker and working his way to becoming Warehouse Manager. Being promoted to Warehouse Manager at the start of the COVID-19 global pandemic gave Connor many new changes to navigate. For one, Renee began reporting directly to Connor after being a lateral coworker from a different department for nearly three years. Renee had been with the company for almost five years, working as a Stocker, supporting herself through college. She had recently graduated with a Bachelor of Science degree in Information

15

Technology and was very grateful for the flexibility the company gave her during her time there. Connor and Renee had a pleasant working relationship over the years and adjusted fairly well to the shift in power dynamics when she began reporting to him.

However, tensions were rising in the workplace. The changes the pandemic rang in were plentiful; folks were reevaluating where they spent their time and energy, and new rules and restrictions affected everyone, at least to some extent.

When Renee walked into the Warehouse at 8:23 am, Connor decided to move forward with a written warning ("write-up") for Renee. As company policy stated, after three unexcused tardies within a pay period, disciplinary action should be taken. Renee was shocked and dismayed as this write-up was handed to her following a disclosure of personal challenges to HR just days prior. Not to mention, she feared the warning may lead to a suspension or termination. While the reassurance from HR that it was "just a warning" helped initially, the vulnerability Renee showed by revealing her personal circumstances now left her feeling ashamed and unsupported by her company.

Connor, on the other hand, believed he was merely doing his job by issuing the write-up and wasn't aware of Renee's discussion with HR. In his mind, he was just following company policy. Nevertheless, the event triggered Renee to make an informal complaint to HR, which included allegations against Connor for deferential treatment and mismanagement.

This is how the conflict started, and it only grew more complex. Stay tuned at the end of each chapter to learn how we intervened and what approaches we took to improve the dynamic.

CHAPTER 2

Psychological Safety

Psychological safety is the degree to which an employee feels safe to speak their mind, be bold, and risk failure in order to better serve the organization. When employees do not feel safe to be themselves or to make mistakes, they will walk on eggshells, never give feedback, and let important issues fester for fear of bringing them to leaders' attention. This is a major breeding ground for intense conflict.

Think for a moment about a time you did not speak up in your workplace even though you knew you had a good idea or some information that could benefit the organization. We've all been there. But why? Because when we speak up, we put ourselves at risk: *What if people don't like my idea? What if it causes conflict? What if it exposes a mistake I made? What if this ruins my chance at a promotion?*

Successful organizations thrive off of innovation; innovation, in turn, thrives off of a healthy competition of ideas. If a company fails to create a psychologically safe place for its employees—a workplace culture wherein individuals feel comfortable speaking their minds and taking risks—it stands to reason that the company will have a harder time innovating and, thus, achieving its goals. Naturally, this type of environment also impacts employee morale, satisfaction, and retention.

According to previous research[1,2], a psychologically safe workplace has many benefits, including:

- Increased innovation
- Better work products
- Greater employee satisfaction and well-being
- Boosted morale
- Less employee turnover
- More creative problem-solving

To truly feel psychologically safe in a workplace (or in any group for that matter), people must feel like they can fail or make mistakes, learn from their mistakes, and still be valued as members of the organization.

Have you ever had something valuable to contribute to your team, yet for some reason or another, chose to withhold

[1] Carmeli, A., Reiter-Palmon, R., & Ziv, E. (2010). Inclusive leadership and employee involvement in creative tasks in the workplace: The mediating role of psychological safety. *Creativity Research Journal, 22(3)*, 250-260. https://doi.org/10.1080/10400419.2010.504654

[2] Frazier, M. L., Fainshmidt, S., Klinger, R. L., Pezeshkan, A., & Vracheva, V. (2017). Psychological safety: A meta-analytic review and extension. *Personnel Psychology, 70(1)*, 113-165.

it? If you have, you're not alone. Multiple studies[3,4] have suggested that between 50-70% of the workforce can recall a time they didn't speak up, even though what they had to offer would've benefited the organization.

The reason we do this is simple human nature: By not speaking up, we receive an immediate personal benefit, a sense of relief, because we're stopping ourselves from having to be vulnerable. And even if we know being vulnerable can be a *good* thing, most of us would rather avoid it—or at least reserve our vulnerability for relationships and settings in which it's likely to be reciprocated or rewarded.

Putting our ideas out there for our colleagues to scrutinize requires a degree of personal risk. The problem is that when we withhold our ideas to avoid being vulnerable, we end up putting our team and organization in a vulnerable position instead. We end up acting out of self-interest, as opposed to working towards a common goal.

In an environment that is not psychologically safe, employees have to choose between their own interests and the company's interests. But what if employees didn't have to choose? What if employees viewed the organization's

---

[3] Xu, A., Ayub, A., & Iqbal, S. (2022). "When" and "why" employees resort to remain silent at work? A moderated mediation model of social undermining. *Journal of Organizational Change Management*.

[4] Milliken, F. J., Morrison, E. W., & Hewlin, P. F. (2003). An exploratory study of employee silence: Issues that employees don't communicate upward and why. *Journal of management studies*, 40(6), 1453-1476.

interests as aligned with their own? If we want to move toward that type of culture, we need to better understand some of the other forces at play. So, what are the factors that make psychological safety so difficult to achieve?

One place to begin is VUCA, an acronym coined by the U.S. Army War College. It stands for:

- **Volatility,** or rapid, unpredictable changes in the environment
- **Uncertainty,** when it comes to thinking about the present or future
- **Complexity,** meaning overly complex systems or structures that create confusion or chaos
- **Ambiguity**, where there is a lack of information or clarity about how to proceed

These forces often run rampant in organizations, especially during times of change, such as reorganization, budget cuts, and turnover in leadership. Suppose individuals already feel like they have to choose between their own interests and those of the organization. In that case, VUCA forces tend to have an amplifying effect, intensifying the threat posed by vulnerability and suppressing an employee's appetite for risk. In any dynamic organization, and especially in workplaces, VUCA is at play on some level.

Why are we painting this picture for you? It's not to make you feel hopeless about cultivating psychologically safe workplace cultures. Rather, it's to help demonstrate that psychologically safe workplaces don't create themselves. Basic psychology and the nature of the workplace inherently undermine psychological safety. So, we as Peaceful Leaders need to be intentional and consistent when it comes to cultivating and maintaining psychological safety.

How do we do that? We'll start by using our awareness of VUCA forces to our own benefit. It is unlikely we can remove these forces entirely. But we can do our best to limit them while responding in ways that promote psychological safety. We've dubbed our approach VUCA^2 [see Figure 2], because for each negative VUCA force, we're responding with two positive forces of our own.

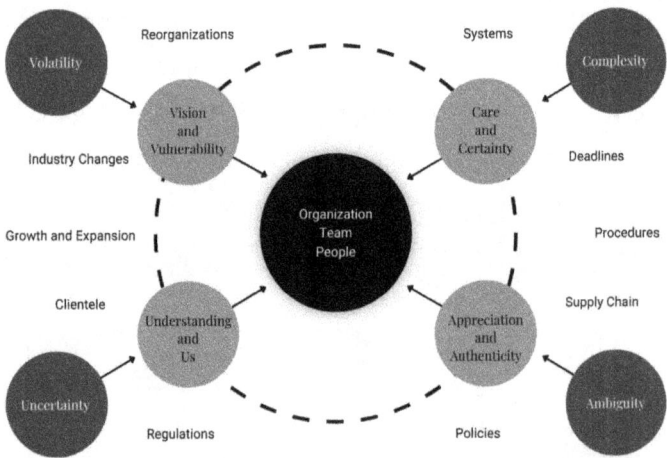

Vision and Vulnerability

When leaders articulate a clear vision for the organization's future, it can serve as a beacon of hope that guides employees through uncertain and volatile times. This shared sense of direction can help employees feel more connected to each other and the organization. It also provides a framework for decision-making that aligns with the organization's mission and values.

Vulnerability is also essential for leaders to model and promote in their organizations. When leaders are willing to be vulnerable, they show their employees that it is safe to take risks, make mistakes, and speak up. This creates an environment where employees feel empowered to share their ideas and opinions without fear of retribution or ridicule. When employees feel safe to be vulnerable, they are more likely to take ownership of their work and collaborate with their colleagues to achieve shared goals.

Simon Sinek, in his TED Talk[5], "Why Good Leaders Make You Feel Safe," talks about an organizational CEO who, during the Great Recession in 2009, decided to introduce a furlough program instead of layoffs. The CEO presented the furlough program by saying, "This is an uncertain time for all of us, but it is better that we all suffer a little so none of us suffers a lot." The *volatility* of the situation could easily have

[5] Sinek, S (2014). Why good leaders feel safe. TED. Retrieved from: https://www.youtube.com/watch?v=lmyZMtPVodo

decimated employee morale and promoted self-interest throughout the organization. But the CEO responded with equal parts *vulnerability* and *vision*, acknowledging the "uncertain time" while offering a clear path forward. In turn, employees self-organized to create a furlough swap program so those who could afford to work less could take on more furlough days. As a result, company morale actually improved in spite of the recession.

Understanding and Us

Understanding requires engaging curiosity and actively seeking to understand the perspectives and experiences of team members. This can involve asking questions and actively listening to feedback, which can help leaders provide better support to their team during difficult times. By creating a culture of curiosity and openness, leaders can encourage their employees to speak up and share their ideas and concerns without fear of judgment or retaliation.

Creating a sense of Us is also essential for building a psychologically safe workplace. We define this as a leader emphasizing a team mindset rather than an individualistic one. By doing this, leaders can foster a shared identity and purpose that motivates employees to work together towards a common goal. This can create a strong sense of support and solidarity, which can be especially important during times of uncertainty and change. By emphasizing the importance of teamwork and collaboration, leaders can help employees feel more confident and secure in their roles, leading to higher engagement and productivity. To better comprehend Understanding and Us, let's look at an example from one of our Peaceful Leader's, Jen, who manages a marketing team at a software company struggling to meet its targets due to a new competitor disrupting the industry.

Jen saw that her team was feeling stressed and overwhelmed and wanted to create a psychologically safe environment where they could share their concerns and ideas. She set up one-on-one meetings with each team member to ask them how they were feeling and what challenges they were facing. She listened carefully to their responses and took notes to ensure she remembered their concerns. Jen also brought the team together as a whole to emphasize collaboration and mutual support for a brainstorming session to generate ideas on how they can work together to overcome their challenges and support each other to mitigate individual stress. Jen's use of Understanding and Us created increased psychological safety, and her team felt more empowered to share their concerns and ideas to achieve their goals during the volatile period.

Care and Certainty

In times of volatility, uncertainty, complexity, and ambiguity (VUCA), it's crucial for leaders to respond with care and empathy to their team members. A Peaceful Leader should acknowledge their team's challenges and offer support to help them navigate difficult times. This can involve demonstrating compassion and empathy when team members take risks and fail. Leaders can foster a culture of innovation and creativity by providing a supportive environment where employees feel safe to take risks and speak up.

Uncertainty is one of the greatest threats to psychological safety. It can lead to anxiety, fear, and a sense of helplessness. In times of high uncertainty, Peaceful Leaders can help their team members feel more secure by identifying areas of certainty and anchoring them in what they know to be true. This can involve focusing on the elements within their power to control and developing a clear action plan that gives team members agency over the situation. By providing a sense of certainty and direction, leaders can reduce fear and anxiety and create a sense of stability that allows team members to work through the unknowns together. Let's look at an example of Care and Certainty from Lars, who manages a team of engineers at a tech startup.

Like many companies in 2020, Lars's company faced uncertainty due to the COVID-19 pandemic, and Lars could tell that his team was anxious and stressed. To build a sense of psychological safety, Lars showed his care and empathy to his team through weekly check-ins to ask how they were doing and offer support. He kept meeting with his team regularly to serve as a reminder to his team that he was a resource for them. Lars also created a sense of certainty for his team by identifying the areas of the company's operations that were within their control and developed a plan of action for the team to rally behind. In tandem, he coached his team to identify where they have control individually over their work and to focus their energy on those areas when they felt stressed. By helping his team feel cared for and empowered to focus on what they have control over, overall stress decreased, which contributed to more focus on team objectives.

Appreciation and Authenticity

Appreciative acknowledgement is another tool a leader can use to foster a psychologically safe culture. By recognizing and appreciating employees' efforts and reframing failures or mistakes as learning opportunities, leaders can encourage employees to take risks and speak up without fear of retaliation or ridicule. This can help promote a culture of trust and transparency where employees feel empowered to share their ideas and contribute to the organization's success. For Peaceful Leaders, authenticity involves being honest and transparent, acting with an ethical mind, and being true to oneself in all aspects of their leadership.

When leaders acknowledge and appreciate their team from an authentic place, it creates a sense of trust and credibility among their team members. Most people can tell when someone else is being genuine rather than fake; authenticity draws people to you, while inauthenticity tends to push people away (even if they're not consciously aware of why they are driven away). In addition to feeling truly valued when authentically appreciated, employees are more likely to feel comfortable speaking up and sharing their ideas when they know their leaders are being genuine and truthful. That's because they know they will get an honest response to their ideas, rather than fake praise or consideration.

Let's look at an example of appreciation and authenticity from one of our Peaceful Leader's, Blair, who manages a team of sales representatives at a retail company. Blair's team was experiencing decreased sales due to a downturn in the economy. As a result, more stress and more conflict among team members started to occur, mostly around blaming each other for sales not going through. In an effort to increase psychological safety, Blair set up weekly team meetings to recognize team members' contributions and to acknowledge demonstrations of what she called "wild sales tactics that almost worked." She asked each sales team member to come to the meeting with a wild sales tactic they experimented with to try and close a sale. The team was able to laugh and celebrate bold actions that often led to failures, which Blair was able to reframe into learning opportunities.

This was only successful because Blair was operating in an authentic manner. In fact, Blair would always start the meeting out with a failure on her part, which helped her team feel comfortable and confident sharing their own wild sales tactics and failures. By speaking from an authentic place, Blair created a culture of trust and transparency that empowered her team members to take ownership of their work and collaborate towards shared goals.

Case Narrative: Psychological Safety

Renee had a difficult time coping with the pandemic. Her mental health had taken a toll on her physical health. After going back to the Warehouse following a short, company-wide furlough, Renee's anxiety and depression began to affect her morning routine, resulting in her frequent tardiness. Renee went to HR to disclose her health concerns and request assistance. Through this meeting, Renee learned she could use her FMLA (Family and Medical Leave Act) time to compensate for when she had morning challenges that caused her to arrive late to work. Renee made an arrangement with HR to use her FMLA, which covered her up to 4 days a month. Connor, however, was unclear about the specifics of her special accommodations.

There was clearly **volatility** in this situation, caused by the COVID-19 pandemic, **uncertainty** about its impacts and how long they would last, **complexity** with regards to the company's compensation structure, and **ambiguity** as it pertained to Connor's awareness of the plan created between Renee and HR.

How could Connor use the VUCA[2] tools to promote Psychological Safety for Renee? Here are some ideas we suggested.

Vulnerability and **V**ision	Share with his team his own concerns, fears, or challenges arising from the pandemic and the company's furloughs, followed by his vision for the future: *"I, too, have laid awake concerned about how we move on from here. It will be a struggle, but I am confident that we will learn a lot about ourselves, each other, and our organization through these challenges ahead and be more resilient than ever when this global event is over."*
Understanding and **U**s	Invite open sharing and support. Help the team focus on supporting each other rather than suffering alone. *"These changes will no doubt impact all of us, but we will get through it together. Let's look out for each other and use this opportunity to support each other. If you're experiencing stress from the changes and need support, I want to*

	understand how it's impacting you, and I will do my best to help."
Care and Certainty	Show care by checking in with people one-on-one to see how they're doing. Ground people in the known and what they can control. *"Hey Renee, how are you doing? How are the changes impacting you? Remember that no one's job is at risk, and business is still moving along. No matter what, you can always talk to me if you need extra support."*
Appreciation and Authenticity	Acknowledge the impacts of team members' contributions. Communicate from a genuine place of appreciation. *"Renee, I noticed the other day you took on one of Raul's tasks. I know your plate is full as well. I wanted to let you know that Raul is beyond relieved and that it made a big difference for him. I was also very moved by your gesture."*

After the morning incident, company HR quickly rescinded the write-up. The tensions between Connor and Renee seemed to grow, however. She was now feeling monitored and judged by Connor in a way she hadn't felt before, leading her to keep her distance from Connor and stay quiet around him. And the more she withdrew, the more Connor felt that Renee was disengaged from her job, which caused him to pay more attention to what she was doing, thus creating an unhealthy cycle between the two of them. After a few weeks, Renee decided to write a grievance letter to HR regarding Connor's management practices, how she's attempted to address these with him in the past, and her request of WDP Warehouse's action.

The HR manager brought both of them into her office to have a discussion. Things did not go very well, however. Renee shut down and had trouble speaking her mind, while Connor felt frustrated and now scrutinized and targeted. The HR manager felt somewhat overwhelmed by the situation and could not figure out how to get these two aligned. She asked them both if they would be open to working with an independent HR consultant, someone who might be able to help smooth things out between them, and they both agreed that would be helpful.

Here's where we come in. Our team at Pollack Peacebuilding Systems was engaged to conduct a dialogue and problem-solving process with Connor and Renee—a process we call Peacemaking. In the following chapters' case narrative sections, we will dive into the questions we asked during the Peacemaking program, the dynamics we discovered, and the processes we implemented to help rebuild trust through the lens of Peaceful Leadership.

STRATEGY SESSION

Okay, let's see how you can implement VUCA^2 in your organization to promote psychological safety. See if you can finish the following sentences.

One strategy I could implement to increase psychological safety in my organization/team is…...

The possible benefits to implementing this strategy are......

If I were to implement that strategy, the challenges I might experience are......

To prepare for and navigate any potential challenges, I can......

My first step in implementing this strategy would be......

CHAPTER 3

Employee Trust

Trust is something we all want from others and something we often assume others have in us. Healthy, peaceful, and mutually beneficial relationships rely on mutual trust as a foundation. When individuals in any relationship, including a work relationship, do not trust one another, conflict is inevitable.

So, how often do we pause and reflect on how trust is built? In organizations, **employee trust** positively impacts workplace performance[6], psychological well-being[7], and

---

[6] Brown, S., Gray, D., McHardy, J., & Taylor, K. (2015). Employee trust and workplace performance. *Journal of Economic Behavior & Organization, 116,* 361-378.

[7] Kelloway, E. K., Turner, N., Barling, J., & Loughlin, C. (2012). Transformational leadership and employee psychological well-being: The mediating role of employee trust in leadership. *Work & Stress, 26(1),* 39-55.

work engagement[8]. Through his research, Dr. Joe Folkman, an organizational psychologist and leadership consultant, has shown that trust is one of, if not *the* most significant leadership quality, as it is the one variable that affects every other leadership quality and every employee satisfaction metric[9].

In the workplace, trust is not something we need to strive for unconditionally or absolutely—such a level of trust is rare in any aspect of life, much less in a working environment. That being said, can your employees trust that you will protect and advocate for their interests? Can your employees trust that you will do what you say you'll do? Can your employees trust you to be transparent and honest? Can they trust you won't take their ideas and present them as your own? Can they trust you'll take responsibility for your own actions? Can they trust you to behave with integrity and predictability?

When it comes to leadership in the workplace, this is the type of trust employees are looking for. The more employees trust you in these ways, the more likely they'll be to serve the organization to the best of their abilities. Equally important, when work challenges or conflicts arise, this mutual trust will

---

[8] Maximo, N., Stander, M. W., & Coxen, L. (2019). Authentic leadership and work engagement: The indirect effects of psychological safety and trust in supervisors. *SA Journal of Industrial Psychology, 45(1)*, 1-11.

[9] Folkman, J. (2022). *The Trifecta of Trust.* River Grove Books.

provide a solid foundation for difficult conversations and constructive resolutions.

In an organizational context, there are four aspects of trust that we should be intentional about cultivating as Peaceful Leaders: task competency trust, accountability trust, professional behavior trust, and position of power trust. This is what we call the T.A.P.P. model of trust. When an organization has established all four of these TAPP elements, a foundation is built in our working relationships that allow employees to handle difficult situations and conflicts in a peaceful manner.

TAPP Model

T	A	P	P
Task Competency-	**Accountability-**	**Professional Behavior-**	**Position of Power-**
Can we trust each other to do our work, meet our deadlines, and do quality work?	Can we trust each other to take responsibility for our own actions and follow through on our commitments?	Can we trust each other to act in a consistent, predictable, and constructive manner?	Can we trust each other to not abuse our positions of power for personal gain?
Tips • Start out small • Set clear expectations on the process • Establish clear KPI's	**Tips** • Be humble and acknowledge your shortcomings • Only commit to things you can follow through on • Set other people up for success	**Tips** • Be consistent and predictable • Pause before responding • Gather information before making decisions	**Tips** • Be transparent • Empower, don't overpower • Share your power

Let's take a look at how we can build these levels of trust. Keep in mind: building trust is a two-way street—for others to trust us, we have to trust others.

Task Competency Trust

Task competency trust is the extent to which others feel confident that we can satisfactorily do our jobs and fulfill our roles as leaders. Here are a few important tips for building task competency trust.

1. Start out small.

   To build trust in your staff, especially new team members or those you feel you cannot fully trust, start by assigning them small tasks. Once you've established a bit of trust, you can gradually move on to more complex tasks, allowing your trust in them to grow. This, in turn, will help them feel more autonomous, competent, and supported while they grow—all of which builds reciprocal trust in you as their leader. If the roles are reversed, you can help others build trust in you by suggesting a small task that you know you can accomplish.

2. Set clear expectations.

   What is it that needs to be completed? When does it need to be completed? What will happen if something unexpected comes up that prevents the task from being completed? How will the two of you communicate about task progress? Clearly outlining these expectations will engender trust in the process, which can scaffold the growth of your trust in one another.

3. Establish clear KPI's.

It's probably fair to say that both you and your team member(s) will want the task to be completed—and completed successfully. But what does success and completion mean? Even if you start small, and even if you set clear expectations, if you both have a different idea of what success and achievement look like, then you are setting yourself up for disappointment on the project while also undermining the trust between you and your team member(s) in the process. To avoid this, make sure everyone involved clearly understands the desired, specific outcomes as well as each milestone along the way.

Accountability Trust

Accountability trust is the extent to which others feel confident that we will take responsibility for our actions and follow through on commitments. Here are a few essential tips for building accountability trust.

1. <u>Be humble and acknowledge your shortcomings.</u>

   Take a moment and think of a time when someone close to you tried to deflect blame or refused to take ownership over something that was clearly their fault. You were probably disappointed or frustrated, right? Others feel the same way when we don't take responsibility for our actions. When you're at fault, try to reframe it in terms of responsibility. Nobody wants to be at fault, of course. But taking responsibility for our actions, especially our failures, is an admirable trait worth striving for—and one that allows others to have trust in our integrity.

2. <u>If you make a commitment, make sure you can follow through.</u>

   Most of us want to say "yes" to everything. But if we agree to do things that aren't feasible for us, we end up damaging the relationship, and the other person loses trust in us. Sometimes, saying "no" is the most respectful thing you can do. At the very least, set clear expectations on a timeline, then make sure to meet the deadline or update the timeline as soon as you recognize you may not hit your target date.

3. <u>Set other people up for success.</u>

   To help you build trust in others, be resolute about your expectations regarding accountability. If your employee agrees to take on extra work, but you can sense they're hesitant to accept, try to understand early on if they can really commit to the task. Sometimes, in relationships where one person has more power than the other, people agree to things without realizing they have a choice. It is incumbent upon a Peaceful Leader to address their employees' hesitations and set them up for success—not only for the benefit of the organization but also to establish a sense of mutual trust.

Professional Behavior Trust

Professional behavior trust is the extent to which others feel confident that we act in a consistent, predictable, and constructive manner. Here are a few important tips for building professional behavior trust.

1. <u>Be consistent and predictable.</u>

   Imagine a supervisor commends an employee who took the initiative to reach out to a client directly to resolve an issue on their account. Then, two weeks later, the supervisor takes an employee off an account for the same behavior. Do you think the employees will be able to trust that supervisor? This kind of inconsistency creates mistrust and puts employees on edge, forcing them to question how to operate within the team. To maintain employee trust, it's important to be consistent and predictable in your actions and communication.

2. Pause before responding.

    Pausing and reflecting on how to respond before doing so will help you become more intentional, consistent, and predictable with your professional behavior. (You will learn a specific process on how to do this when you get to the Patience Competency later on in the book.)

3. Gather information before making decisions.

    If your go-to strategy is to gather information and seek different perspectives when problems arise, you will automatically create space between the situation and your response. Not only will having more information help you respond more predictably, but it will also help you avoid making impulsive and reactive decisions that may lead to conflict.

Position of Power Trust

1. Be transparent.

    When you have to make difficult decisions as a leader, people will likely question whether you have the best interests of others in mind. Consequently, it's important to be as transparent as possible in your decision-making process—this will prevent people from making unfavorable assumptions about your motives.

2. <u>Empower, don't overpower.</u>

As a leader, you agree to work for and protect the interests of those you lead. With that comes a social contract regarding your use of power. When it comes to working with your team, lead by empowering, not overpowering. As soon as you start to overpower, you will lose trust in your team. And if they continue to follow you, it will be out of fear and compliance rather than respect and trust.

3. <u>Share your power.</u>

Let your team in on the decision-making process if an important decision needs to be made. If you are part of a committee and can't make a meeting, send a team member in your stead to take notes and represent the team's interests. Even these small examples of sharing power communicate to your team that you trust them; in return, they'll likely end up building trust in you. (Inclusive decision-making is a topic we will cover thoroughly later in this book.)

The TAPP Trust Framework, which includes Task Trust, Accountability Trust, Professional Behavior Trust, and Position of Power Trust, is crucial for building employee trust in the workplace. Task Trust builds confidence that our employees' work products will be of high quality and completed on time. Accountability Trust ensures that the team can count on each other and you as a leader to follow through with your commitments and that there is shared understanding that each individual takes ownership of their own actions and decisions. Professional Behavior Trust is built when we act consistently, predictably, and constructively, even when stressed. The position of Power Trust requires leaders to use their authority responsibly and in service to the team. When leaders use their position of power for their own personal gain at the expense of the team, that leader will lose their employee's trust.

Remember that trust is something that a leader needs in their team and that a team needs in their leader. Trust is built over time; every week and every day is an opportunity to create or lose trust with your team. A Peaceful Leader will consciously and consistently build trust with their team through the TAPP Trust Framework, which can improve communication, collaboration, and job satisfaction, leading to increased productivity and greater likelihood of organizational success.

Case Narrative: Employee Trust

Connor wasn't a big fan of using profanity in the Warehouse. While it wasn't necessarily a rule not to, most of the team refrained from vulgar language when Connor was around. Renee was aware of this but started to notice that some staff members were nonchalantly throwing around "the F-bomb" without Connor appearing bothered. Then one day, seeing that someone left the forklift parked in the middle of the aisle, Renee yelled: "What the f**k, guys! You're causing a f***ing hazard!" Connor responded, telling her to watch her language on the floor. His reprimand left Renee feeling embarrassed and singled-out. On top of this, Renee had noticed Connor leaving the warehouse early when something came up with his wife or children—despite the fact that he wrote her up for her tardiness. Considering all this, mistrust was growing between the two; left unattended, it would no doubt lead to escalating conflict.

In looking at the four aspects of trust in the workplace, **task competency trust** appeared to have been cultivated. Connor never felt concerned over Renee's productivity or quality of work. Late or not, he could trust that she wouldn't let her task completion slip. Renee shared this assurance in Connor's reliability and competency. In other words, they had no mistrust about one another's ability to do their jobs well.

Accountability trust began to show up, however, when Renee noticed Connor not being accountable for monitoring others' use of profanity. Connor also was feeling mistrust. At the start of our Peacemaking process, he shared: "During our discussion with HR, Renee said she would be more communicative with me about what she needs. But I haven't heard from her at all, even though she continues to come late sometimes and remains pretty withdrawn." In other words, she was not following through on what she had agreed to.

Additionally, Renee's **position of power trust** and **professional behavior trust** in Connor were also being challenged. She perceived that Connor was abusing his power for personal gain by leaving the Warehouse early when his family's needs arose, yet having an issue with her coming in late when *her* needs arose. Through Renee's lens, Connor's reactive write-up failed to gather information and honor the effective technique of *pausing before response.* Not to mention, his responses to her foul language compared to his responses to her male co-workers' foul language further reinforced her sense that he had different expectations for different employees— leading to a breakdown of the **position of power, professional behavior, and accountability trust.**

This was all important information for us to gather and analyze. Trust is the foundation of relationships, and we would need to understand what types of trust were broken here to create an appropriate program for rebuilding the relationship. Stay tuned at the end of Chapter 4 to learn what we discovered next and how we began addressing the issues.

STRATEGY SESSION

Okay, let's see how you can build trust in your organization. See if you can finish the following sentences.

A relationship that I would like to improve trust in is......

The specific domains of trust (Task Competency, Accountability, Professional Behavior, and Position of Power) that I need to build in this relationship are......

One strategy that I could try that might help improve trust in this relationship is......

Some unexpected challenges that might occur are......

I can navigate those challenges by......

If I were to implement that strategy, I would start by......

CHAPTER 4

Inclusion

Humans are social and tribal creatures. We tend to trust people who are in our tribe more readily than those who are not. Being left out—not feeling like you have a voice, or that you belong, or that you have value—is one of our deepest fears. In the workplace, this happens all the time, in ways big and small. Maybe a colleague forgot to invite you to an office happy hour; maybe you weren't consulted in a business decision that directly impacted your work. Regardless of the situation, when we're relegated to the margins or left out of the loop, we tend to feel a lack of control and safety and react from a place of self-interest or fear, all of which are potent catalysts for conflict. Such conflict will frequently lead to interpersonal tension, HR complaints, and a high degree of employee turnover. And as we suggested in the section on psychological safety, responding from self-interest can undermine the shared goals of the organization.

Inclusion is about intentionally creating a space for all perspectives so people feel they have belonging, value, purpose, and a voice in the work environment. While the three pillars of Peaceful Leadership overlap and reinforce each other in different ways, inclusion serves as the glue that holds them all together. When employees are made to feel included, they're more likely to experience psychological safety and trust—and, therefore, more willing to put the organization's interests ahead of their own while at work.

Inclusion is important for everyone in the workplace to understand. But it's especially vital for leaders: A recent *Harvard Business Review* article[10] indicated that leaders and supervisors have the greatest influence over whether members of their teams feel included; moreover, having an inclusive leadership style—being open, accessible, and available[11]—has been shown to support feelings of psychological safety[12], engagement[13], and organization-based

---

[10] Bourke, J. & Titus, A. (2020). The Key to Inclusive Leadership. *Harvard Business Review*. Retrieved from: https://hbr.org/2020/03/the-key-to-inclusive-leadership

[11] Carmeli, A., Reiter-Palmon, R., & Ziv, E. (2010). Inclusive leadership and employee involvement in creative tasks in the workplace: The mediating role of psychological safety. *Creativity Research Journal, 22(3),* 250-260.

[12] Nembhard, I. M., & Edmondson, A. C. (2006). Making it safe: The effects of leader inclusiveness and professional status on psychological safety and improvement efforts in health care teams. *Journal of Organizational Behavior, 27(7),* 941-966.

[13] Choi, S. B., Tran, T. B. H., & Park, B. I. (2015). Inclusive leadership and work engagement: Mediating roles of affective organizational commitment

self-esteem[14]. In other words, inclusion has to be established by an organization's leaders. To help you ensure team members are made to feel they belong, we created the BPV^2 model of inclusion for Peaceful Leadership.

---

and creativity. *Social Behavior and Personality: An International Journal, 43(6),* 931-943.

[14] Cottrill, K., Lopez, P. D., & Hoffman, C. C. (2014). How authentic leadership and inclusion benefit organizations. *Equality, Diversity and Inclusion: An International Journal.*

BPV^2

Belonging	⊜	You are an important member of a group	⟩	• Anchor belonging in your culture • Create opportunities for connection • Addressing exclusion immediately
Purpose and **V**alue	⊜	You have a role in the group and that role has purpose and value to the mission of the group	⟩	• Creating clear roles and responsibilities • Connecting work and value • Celebrating people and contributions (no matter how small)
Voice	⊜	You have a say in what the group is doing and where the group is heading	⟩	• Creating opportunities for people to engage • Listening up and follow up • Encouraging diversity in your job application process

Before we discuss some actionable techniques for you as a Peaceful Leader to bring **Belonging**, **Purpose**, **Value**, and **Voice** into your workplace, we should acknowledge that not everyone in our organizations is going to experience inclusion the same way. People with marginalized identities in your organization or limited opportunities for influence are going to experience inclusion—and, moreover, *exclusion*—differently than those who tend to fit in with the workplace culture or have greater access to opportunities.

Race, gender, sexuality, age, beliefs, communication style, worldview, or ability (to name a few) can impact the way someone experiences exclusion, particularly when it is mediated by someone in a position of power within the organization. Reflect on your organization and the people (or positions) who tend to have fewer opportunities to be included or have their voices heard. You may want to consider being extra intentional about creating opportunities for them in specific ways.

Now, let's go over some tips to bring BPV^2 or belonging, purpose, value, and voice into your organization.

Belonging

According to a study by BetterUp.com,[15] employees with a high sense of belonging take 75% fewer sick days than

---

[15] https://hbr.org/2019/12/the-value-of-belonging-at-work

those who feel excluded; they also score 56% better in job performance. In addition, excluded employees have a 50% higher rate of turnover than employees who feel they belong. Here are some tips for bringing belonging into your organization:

1. Anchor belonging in your culture

   Take a look at how your team or organization is structured and identify where belonging is built or created within your organization. Consider if your systems, policies, or procedures leave anyone or any job function out, especially for company communications. For example, perhaps your night shift maintenance crew is not able to attend your company-wide town hall that you have scheduled for the middle of the day. How might you create belonging for those employees to participate? Review available resources like access to professional development funds or company travel opportunities. Consider creating policies and structures for company resources that allow everyone to have clearly defined access to them, even if they are not equal. Anchoring belonging in your organizational structure will support and reinforce your other individual efforts, as well as give clear guidance to team leaders at multiple levels on how to include everyone.

2. <u>Create opportunities for social connection.</u>

    To create social connections in companies, it's important to think inside-out and focus on building connections at both the individual team and company-wide levels. One practical approach is to start by providing opportunities for team members to feel a sense of belonging and connection within their own unit. This can be achieved through team-building activities like team lunches, celebrations of team accomplishments, or creating a dedicated space for staff to mingle on breaks. For example, a team could organize a quarterly team lunch where team members can connect and bond over their shared experiences and goals.

    Once teams and departments have established a sense of belonging, expanding that sense of connection to the company level may be wise. This can be achieved through company-wide events like annual retreats, charity events, and team-building activities that bring employees from different departments together. For example, a company could organize a volunteer charity event where employees from different departments come together to volunteer and give back to the community. By fostering social connections at all levels, companies can create a positive work culture that promotes employee well-being and ultimately leads to increased productivity and success.

3. <u>Address exclusion immediately</u>
   Addressing exclusion in the workplace is crucial for creating a sense of belonging and promoting a positive work environment. If you notice individuals being excluded, it's important to act and address the situation immediately. Here are some do's and don'ts to keep in mind:

Do:

- Take responsibility for your and/or your organization's role in the exclusion and commit to closing any system gaps that may have facilitated the exclusion.
- Speak directly with the individuals involved to understand the situation and what contributed to the exclusion. Identify a resolution and demonstrate that you are invested in fostering an inclusive workplace for the folks left out.
- Take action to create a sense of belonging, such as inviting the excluded individuals to join in on team activities, initiating conversations to build relationships, or modifying company policies or procedures.

- Monitor the situation to ensure that the exclusion does not continue. Check in periodically with the people involved.

Don't:

- Ignore the situation and hope it will resolve itself. It most likely won't and may, in fact, get worse or start to impact other areas of the company.
- Blame the excluded individuals for being left out or not fitting in. Instead, try to identify what contributed to the exclusion.
- Allow the exclusion to continue without taking any action. Even if it is only one employee, seek to understand what contributed to the situation. There may be others feeling the same way.
- Downplay the seriousness of the situation. Exclusion can easily lead to increased turnover rates and decreased employee satisfaction with the company.

While it may not be possible to foster a sense of belonging for everyone in the company all the time, addressing exclusion in a timely manner demonstrates to your employees that you care and are committed to creating a positive work environment. By taking responsibility and making immediate changes, you can create a workplace where everyone feels heard and included.

Purpose and Value

Belonging to a group is essential for creating a positive work environment, but it's not enough on its own. If employees feel like they belong but don't have a clear sense of purpose or feel like they're not providing value to the organization, they may become disengaged. Here are some tips to help employees feel more connected and engaged:

1. <u>Create clear roles and responsibilities.</u>

   Clarity on roles and responsibilities is essential for employees to be able to identify their purpose in the organization. Employees should be able to clearly articulate what they do and how it contributes to the organization's mission. This can be done through job descriptions, regular employee reviews, and one-on-one check-ins.

2. <u>Connect work and value.</u>

   Help your team members see the impact of their work. Give feedback regularly to individuals and to the team to help employees connect their day-to-day work with its impact on the organization. For example, if it is someone's job to complete a report on time, let them know the impact timeliness has on the team or the organization's overarching objective. This may help them reframe a potentially mundane task into a fulfilling and irreplaceable element of the larger group effort.

3. <u>Celebrate people and their contributions (no matter how small)</u>
    Take time out of your week to celebrate the work your team is doing. Do individual callouts for exceptional performance. Celebrate anniversaries and birthdays so people know you're thinking of them. Create a recognition board so employees get to know other team members and how they contribute. No matter how small the task or success, find ways to celebrate wins, accomplishments, and individual efforts.

As a Peaceful Leader, an essential part of your job is helping your team members feel important and valued. Brainstorm three ways you can help your team feel purpose and value at your company. Small, consistent efforts are often more meaningful for employees than large, infrequent gestures or proclamations.

Voice

Belonging is the foundation for inclusion. Purpose and providing value for the company are equally important for a sense of being part of the team. The next level for inclusion is to give employees a voice to participate in the direction of the company or about their experience as an employee. Having a voice gives people some level of control over their environment by contributing to the direction of the company or decisions that might impact them. Here are a few tips for giving team members a voice.

1. <u>Create opportunities for people to engage.</u>
   Creating opportunities for people to engage is crucial for promoting a positive work environment and empowering employees. Here are some ideas on how to promote engagement:

   - Regular 1-on-1 meetings: Set aside time to meet with each member of your team individually to discuss their goals, progress, and concerns. This provides a safe space for employees to share their thoughts and gives you an opportunity to provide guidance and support.
   - Organizational assessments: Organizational or team assessments can give your employees an anonymous means to share their perspectives without fear of retaliation. Depending on your company size, you may want to facilitate an organizational assessment every couple of years.
   - Committees and work groups: Give employees an opportunity to be involved in work groups or committees to advance company-wide initiatives.

- Cross-functional and cross-hierarchy collaboration: Create systems or programs to encourage employees to step outside of their own job-function or department. This can help build relationships that might not otherwise be created, serve as internal professional development opportunities, and facilitate a better understanding of their role in the company. Consider initiatives like job shadowing or rotation, mentoring programs, and creating cross-functional sub-teams.

- Town halls and focus groups: Allow employees to share their thoughts and opinions on decisions that impact them through town halls and focus groups to gather perspective and feedback.

Remember, the goal is to give people at all levels of the organization a voice and to create a culture of openness, transparency, and collaboration. You can create a workplace where everyone feels heard and valued by consistently engaging with employees and providing opportunities for input and feedback.

2. Listen up and follow up.
Providing avenues for employees to give feedback is an essential first step. However, proper follow-up after receiving feedback is equally important. Here

are some tips for how to effectively follow up with employees after receiving feedback:

- Show that you listened: Ask questions for clarification if necessary, and make sure you have a complete understanding of their concerns and suggestions. Summarize back the main points you heard to ensure clarity, which also lets them know that you understood their feedback well enough to put it into your own words.

- Make changes where appropriate: While you don't need to adopt every piece of feedback, you should act where appropriate.

- Follow up with your team: Once you've made changes, and especially when you don't make any changes from the feedback, it's essential to let your team know what changes you made or didn't make and why you implemented or did not implement the feedback you received. Explain your thought process as appropriate so they aren't left wondering why you didn't follow all of their feedback.

- Continue the dialogue: Following up on feedback is not a one-time event. It's important to continue soliciting feedback from employees, make changes accordingly, and follow-up regularly with updates or new information to keep everyone in the loop on important decisions.

Remember, employees will stop speaking up if they don't feel their feedback is being heard and acted upon. By listening to feedback, making changes, and following up with your team, you can build a culture of trust and openness where employees feel valued and heard.

3. <u>Encourage diversity in your job application process</u>
Encouraging diversity in your job application process is an important step toward creating a more inclusive workplace. Here are some tips to keep in mind:

- Include diverse perspectives as an attribute in the hiring process: Hiring managers are just as susceptible to affinity bias as anyone else. Affinity bias is a tendency to see people more favorably when they are more like us, which can influence hiring managers. Consider having diverse perspectives as a metric for hiring managers to consider in the hiring process, along with diverse education, experience, and skills. This will increase the likelihood that your team doesn't become an echo chamber susceptible to groupthink and blind spots.

- Encourage diversity in leadership positions: It's especially important to encourage candidates with diverse experiences and perspectives to apply for leadership positions. Having diverse perspectives in leadership positions can help promote representation for more elements of your workforce.

- Partner with a diverse set of organizations or schools: Partnering with organizations in and outside your community or industry can help you promote job openings to communities and professionals who might not normally see your job postings. This can help increase the variety of perspectives and backgrounds of your applicant pool and ensure that your organization is reaching a wider audience.

- Avoid hiring based on diversity alone: While it's important to promote diversity in your hiring process, avoid hiring based solely on diversity. This can easily lead to your existing employees feeling excluded or not valued for their contributions and qualifications, which can result in decreased morale, belonging, and employee retention. Instead, prioritize hiring candidates who are the best fit for the job, which should take into consideration applicants who will bring unique perspectives and experiences to the organization.

Just like psychological safety and employee trust, inclusion is not something that happens automatically—it is intentionally cultivated. As you continue through the chapters covering the PLT Core Competencies, consider how you might use them to intentionally cultivate a culture of inclusion.

Case Narrative: Inclusion

Even though Connor had been promoted to a leadership position, he still felt like he was just part of the crew and strived to ensure everyone felt included in decisions that might affect them. They were a team of equals, in his mind. It never dawned on Connor that his position of power might inherently change things, regardless of how he felt internally.

Not being aware of how his actions as a leader might be perceived created a few issues. For example, Connor did not schedule any regular all-team meetings, but sometimes, when Connor noticed the majority of the team was around, he would spontaneously ask for "a round-up" to check in with everyone. These sporadic "team meetings" happened a few times when Renee was not present, leading to her perception that she was being left out intentionally. As one of only three females in the warehouse, she began to believe she was being left out due to being a woman, which made her feel like she did not **belong** in the tribe. Was Connor aware of this?

From Renee's perspective, she had addressed this issue with Connor directly in the past. From Connor's perspective, he had no clue! So, was the exclusion **addressed**, with an action plan to **follow-up?** Unfortunately, no. As an emerging leader, thrown into a management position without proper training, Connor was learning these best practices the hard way, which is sometimes the best or only way to learn.

During our intervention, we helped Connor understand the way his decisions and actions may be perceived through the lens of power. The team's assumptions about Connor's intentions were being magnified and scrutinized now, even unconsciously, due to the power dynamic inherent in leadership. We explored how he might create more structured opportunities for people to engage and share feedback, such as in regularly scheduled—rather than spontaneous—meetings. This way, everyone could be included, and misperceptions about exclusion would be mitigated. During such meetings, it would be important for Connor to ask questions and listen more than talk. And based on what he hears, he would have to make an effort to check-in or follow up with folks about what they need, what they're working on, and/or how they could use support. **Listening up** and **following up** are absolute requisites for *psychological safety, trust,* and *inclusion.*

STRATEGY SESSION

Okay, let's see how you can build inclusive practices in your organization. See if you can finish the following sentences.

One strategy I could implement to promote inclusion in my organization / team is......

The possible benefits to implementing this strategy are......

If I were to implement that strategy, the challenges I might experience are.....

To prepare for and navigate any potential challenges, I can......

My first step in implementing this strategy would be......

CHAPTER 5

Patience

Now that we have established a clear understanding of the three core pillars of Peaceful Leadership, we can dive into the model's five core competencies. It is through these competencies and the critical skills that embody them that we can establish the core pillars in our organizations.

The first competency, **patience**, refers to one's ability to remain calm in challenging circumstances[16]. Although sometimes measured in the organizational literature as simply trusting in one's organization and the decision-making processes in place[17], a more proactive view of patience is that it involves effectively coping with difficult or

---

[16] Kumar, V., & Dhiman, S. (2022). Transcending Emerging Barriers Through Patience. In *Innovative Leadership in Times of Compelling Changes* (pp. 79-98). Springer, Cham.

[17] Hagedoorn, M., Van Yperen, N. W., Van de Vliert, E., & Buunk, B. P. (1999). Employees' reactions to problematic events: A circumplex structure of five categories of responses, and the role of job satisfaction. *Journal of Organizational Behavior, 20(3),* 309-321.

trying circumstances[18]. Leaders learn to exhibit patience through self-regulation, by which they "draw upon their experience to respond in a way that takes into account the implications of their actions, harnessing emotional reactions rather than exhibiting impulsive and/or agitated behaviors that might backfire or otherwise pose troublesome consequences"[3].

Researchers have found patience exhibited by leaders in the workplace improves employee well-being, empathy, compassion, and harmony[18]. In this chapter, we will discuss the skills we have found to be essential in embodying patience in the workplace. These include emotional intelligence, self-regulation, creating your circle of control, and receiving feedback effectively.

[18] Comer, D. R., & Sekerka, L. E. (2014). Taking time for patience in organizations. *Journal of Management Development, 33(1)*, 6-23.

Emotional Intelligence

Across a wide array of research, emotional intelligence has been shown to have a positive effect on conflict resolution strategies[19,20]team performance,[21] and leader effectiveness.[22] The more emotionally intelligent you are, the more patient and intentional you'll be in your responses and actions—thereby promoting the three pillars of Peaceful Leadership.

You probably have a pretty good sense of what emotional intelligence means. But for purposes of this book, let's get specific. According to Daniel Goleman, who popularized the term, we can think of emotional intelligence as being composed of four basic elements [see Figure 5]:

- Self-awareness
- Self-regulation
- Relationship-awareness
- Relationship-navigation

[19] Jordan, P. J., & Troth, A. C. (2002). Emotional intelligence and conflict resolution: Implications for human resource development. *Advances in developing human resources*, 4(1), 62-79.

[20] Rahim, M. A., Psenicka, C., Polychroniou, P., Zhao, J. H., Yu, C. S., Chan, K. A., ... & van Wyk, R. (2002). A model of emotional intelligence and conflict management strategies: A study in seven countries. *The International journal of organizational analysis.*

[21] Jordan, P. J., & Troth, A. C. (2004). Managing emotions during team problem solving: Emotional intelligence and conflict resolution. *Human performance*, 17(2), 195-218.

[22] Kerr, R., Garvin, J., Heaton, N., & Boyle, E. (2006). Emotional intelligence and leadership effectiveness. *Leadership & Organization Development Journal.*

	Awareness	**Regulation/Navigation**
Self	**Self-Awareness** *Understanding your emotional experience* • Reflection and self-examination • Aware of biases • Knowing your triggers and needs	**Self-Regulation** *How your emotions are regulated before you respond* • Responding, not reacting • Pause and breathe • Respond from place of control
Relationships	**Relationship-Awareness** *Understanding the emotional experience of others* • Empathy and compassion • Willing to listen and understand • Organizational awareness • Be curious	**Relationship-Navigation** *How to respond to relational dynamics in a healthy way* • Inspire and motive • Coach and Mentor • Make amends and resolve conflict • Promote teamwork and collaboration

Self-awareness is the ability to be aware of and understand one's own emotional experiences. The emotional center of our brain is much stronger and more developed than our rational and critical thinking pathways. Awareness of our emotional experience puts us in a better position for self-regulation.

Self-regulation is the ability to stay in control of one's actions, behaviors, and communications, as opposed to letting emotions dictate how one responds. Emotional reactions often lead to unintended outcomes and can easily start or escalate conflict.

Relationship-awareness is an awareness of the emotional experience of others—in particular, the ability to recognize the impact your actions or communications have on those around you. A Peaceful Leader must be at least somewhat aware of people's emotional experiences around them if they are to understand how to best navigate relationships in the workplace.

Relationship-navigation is the ability to navigate relationships, resolve conflicts, be empathetic, provide support, make amends, inspire confidence, and increase morale. Relationship-navigation is the culmination of self-awareness, self-regulation, and relationship-awareness.

Much of this chapter will focus on self-awareness and self-regulation. Once we can confidently be self-aware and self-regulate, we can strive to develop relationship-awareness and relationship-navigation. (Relationship-awareness and relationship-navigation will be covered more thoroughly in the other Core Competency chapters.)

Self-awareness and self-regulation are most important during times of stress or heightened emotional experiences. So, before we discuss those two elements of emotional intelligence, let's go over the two ways that we experience stress and the impacts each has on how we respond.

Eustress is the kind of stress that motivates and energizes us. We can view it as positive stress, which typically satisfies or exercises one of our RISC needs: respect, identity, safety, or control. For example, if you get a well-earned promotion, you may experience extra stress in navigating that transition, but the stressful situation makes you feel respected, increases your sense of purpose, or gives you more control or autonomy over your work. You may also feel extra motivated and energized by the stress of the new job, which can even elevate your performance.

Distress, on the other hand, is the type of stress most of us mean when we think about stress. Distress occurs when we experience events that undermine or disrupt our psychological needs. For example, if your supervisor assigns you an overwhelming number of projects and tasks, you may feel like you've lost control or that your time is not being respected, causing you to experience distress. In this state of stress, our body ramps up the production of cortisol (the body's stress hormone) and adrenaline, which undermines our immune system, creates an overactive amygdala (the emotional center of our brain) and inhibits communication to our prefrontal cortex (the rational center of our brain). This is what's commonly known as the "fight or flight" response.

When we respond from a place of *distress*, we tend to do so from a place of fear, which often results in fight/flight behavior, such as lashing out, despondence, or avoidance. In situations like these, it may look to others like we are the ones causing the problem, avoiding taking responsibility for our actions, not willing to resolve issues, or unable to let go of the past.

Peaceful Leaders should do their best to be patient and respond from a place of care, collaboration, and curiosity. When we respond with care, collaboration, and curiosity, we can more easily practice self-reflection, ask for feedback before responding, separate the person from the problem, and focus on the future instead of the past.

Self-Regulation with S.T.O.P.

A Peaceful Leader will strive to be in control of their own actions and communications—increasing their patience to help promote the three pillars of psychological safety, employee trust, and inclusion. The more aware we are of our own emotional experiences and stress responses, the more likely we'll be able to maintain control over or regulate our actions and communications during moments of distress, which might otherwise cause or escalate conflict.

To self-regulate, we can follow a four-step process using the acronym STOP.

STOP

Take a Breath

Take 10 deep breaths to connect your brain with your body

Proceed

Proceed with care, with a positive intention from your circle of control

Stop

Pause before you respond or act to avoid responding from distress or fear

Observe

Observe your EQ Triangle (Thoughts, Physical Sensations, Behaviors) and offer yourself validation

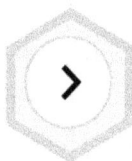

To **stop** and **take a breath** should be fairly easy, but these first two steps are often lost in the flurry of stressful situations. Stopping gives you time to let your rational brain catch up with your emotional brain, while breathing promotes oxygen intake—one of the quickest ways to filter cortisol out of your system. Without creating space between your stress response and your action, the emotional center of your brain is more likely to direct your responses. And remember, the goal is to be in control of our actions and communications—to make them more intentional and deliberate.

Once we have stopped and breathed to create space between the stressor and action, we want to **observe** where our response is coming from. Not only does this provide us with more information on how to **proceed**, but it also helps us become more self-aware about how we respond to stressful and emotional experiences.

When we feel stressed, angry, frustrated, or have any emotional experience, for that matter, we often rely on such emotional labels to describe our experiences. But what information is fueling this emotional label? There are three domains of information we want to observe, which together make up the EQ Triangle: physical sensations, thought patterns, and behaviors.

THOUGHTS
- What judgements or biases do you have?
- Are your thoughts coming from a place of distress and fear or eustress?

PHYSICAL SENSATIONS
- How are you experiencing the emotion / stress in your body?
- Heart rate, breathing, muscle tension, etc.

BEHAVIORS
- What are your actions or communications?
- What are your behavioral and communication impulses?

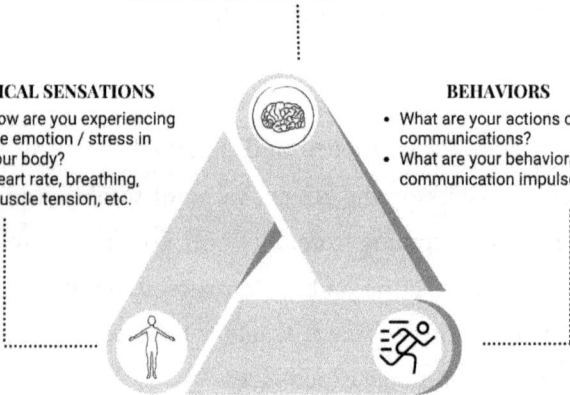

So, let's do a little experiment. Take a moment to think about a situation that was stressful. Try this first with a situation that causes you just a little stress. We don't want to dive into anything too heavy right away. Once you have it in mind and perhaps can feel a bit of stress, proceed with the following observations.

Physical Sensations

Are you experiencing an increase in your heart rate or breathing? Any muscle tension? A flushed face, perspiration, or any other physical response to the emotion or stress? What do these sensations feel like exactly? Do they feel warm/cold? Tingly/throbbing? Might they be associated with a particular color or texture? Try to describe them to yourself. These physical sensations are often the first sign that you are experiencing stress, so becoming more aware of them is important for developing greater self-awareness and self-regulation.

Thought Patterns

When under stress or during an emotional experience, where does your mind go? What biases or judgments are you holding about other people and/or your surrounding environment? Are your thought processes productive and constructive? Or are they causing you more stress and fueling negative self-talk or judgments?

When observing our thoughts, we should pay special attention to certain cognitive biases and errors. One such heuristic is the **fundamental attribution error**—a psychological phenomenon whereby we attribute other people's unproductive behaviors to their character, but we attribute our *own* unproductive behaviors to our external environment. For example, imagine you're driving down the road, and someone is tailgating you. It is likely you will attribute their behavior to their character—being a poor or unsafe driver. But let's say that you are so focused on the car behind you that you don't realize you are tailgating the car in front of *you*. The fundamental attribution error would predict that you would attribute your own behavior not to your driving ability but to the driver distracting you (i.e., your external environment). In other words, you blame others for the kind of behaviors for which you would excuse yourself. This error shows up all the time, particularly in the workplace. Think back: Does the fundamental attribution error apply in any way to the stressful situation you thought about?

Cognitive dissonance is another psychological phenomenon to be aware of. This state explains how humans strive for self-consistency between our beliefs and our behaviors. If you have a belief that one shouldn't interrupt others during meetings, cognitive dissonance would suggest that you are less likely to interrupt others during meetings than someone who doesn't share that belief. As our beliefs change over time, so do our actions, which makes sense. However, our behaviors can also modify our beliefs. For example, if in a meeting you interrupt a colleague because you have something especially important to say, you may modify your belief from "I shouldn't interrupt others in meetings" to "I shouldn't interrupt others in meetings unless I have something really important to say." This type of modification allows us to save face and operate in alignment with our beliefs. In your stressful situation, is there any cognitive dissonance occurring? Have you altered your prevailing beliefs to fit the situation in some way?

Hostile attribution bias is a cognitive bias that highlights our tendency to assign a hostile intention to other people's behaviors. When you are in a meeting, and a colleague interrupts you, the hostile attribution bias may explain your assumption that the individual is trying to undermine you in front of the team. You might surmise that they want to get an edge on you for a promotion you're both interested in, when in reality, their interruption may have a totally different explanation. The hostile attribution bias is typically applied to individuals or the groups they are perceived to represent, with whom you have had at least one negative past experience. In your stressful situation, are you making any assumptions that someone is being hostile when there is a possibility that their behavior could be motivated by something other than hostility?

Confirmation bias is the psychological tendency to notice and consider information that reinforces our beliefs about the world, a situation, or other people and reject information that contradicts our beliefs. For example, if you believe your coworker is unreliable when it comes to meeting deadlines, it's likely you'll notice the times he misses deadlines and count it as evidence to support that belief. However, you will be less likely to recognize or consider the times he does meet his deadlines. Are you paying attention only to evidence that supports your beliefs? Are there any elements of your stressful situation that might contradict your beliefs about the person or event?

Finally, **dichotomous thinking** is a phenomenon that describes our tendency to engage in all-or-nothing or extreme thinking—sometimes called "black and white" thinking. When we engage in dichotomous thinking, we have a hard time considering the gray areas of situations. For example, you may view your direct report's performance on the project as simply positive or negative when perhaps she performed well in some areas and needs improvement in others. In your stressful situation, are you thinking in extremes?

These cognitive biases, or tricks of the mind, occur in all sorts of situations. With regards to your own stressful situation, hopefully, you're starting to see the importance of creating space between the mental-emotional response to situations and your behavioral response. There is a lot to observe and be mindful of!

Behavior

Behavior is the last domain of observation. Our behavior is often influenced by whatever stressor or emotion we are experiencing. So, examining our behaviors and our behavioral tendencies can be useful information for understanding ourselves and how we self-regulate. Regarding your stressful situation, what have been your behavioral responses to the experience so far? What have you felt compelled to do? We've all written emails, sent texts, or said things we wish we could take back.

While observing your behaviors, ask yourself: Are my behaviors constructive or destructive to my goals moving forward? Do they help or harm my relationships? Do they embody patience and help promote the three pillars of Peaceful Leadership? What actions could I have taken instead to promote them?

Now that we understand the importance of creating space between a stressor and an action as a means of improving our self-regulation, we can now proceed. This involves moving from *concern to control* and then from *control to action*.

Creating Your Circle of Control

In Stephen Covey's book, *Seven Habits of Highly Effective People*, he discusses the importance of differentiating between your **circle of concern** and your **circle of control**.

The <u>Circle of Concern</u> is that which is out of our means to change

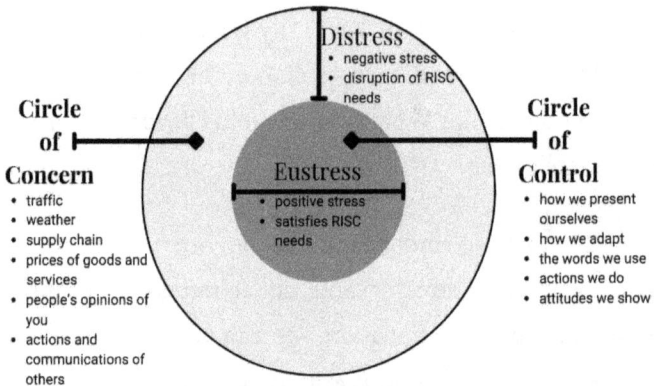

Distress
- negative stress
- disruption of RISC needs

Eustress
- positive stress
- satisfies RISC needs

Circle of Concern
- traffic
- weather
- supply chain
- prices of goods and services
- people's opinions of you
- actions and communications of others

Circle of Control
- how we present ourselves
- how we adapt
- the words we use
- actions we do
- attitudes we show

Our <u>Circle of Control</u> is where we have the power to act or change

This framework is consistent with research concerning the locus of control and well-being, which suggests that the more control people feel they have over their lives, including their work lives, the better they feel across a number of well-being measures.[23,24]

Our circle of concern refers to things about which we're concerned but which we have no control or influence over. Things that might go into our circle of concern include traffic, the weather, changes in the supply chain, prices of other people's goods and services, people's opinions of you, and the actions and communications of others. When we get stuck in our circle of concern, we may feel distressed or afraid. And when we're distressed or afraid, our actions and communications are more likely to come from a place of self-interest and/or result in a fight/flight/freeze response.

Our circle of control, by contrast, refers to things over which we have control or influence. Things that might fall into our circle of control include the time we leave for work in the morning, what clothes we wear, how we adapt to changes in our environment, and our words, attitudes, and actions. When we live in our circle of control, we're more

---

[23] Spector, P. E., Cooper, C. L., Sanchez, J. I., O'Driscoll, M., Sparks, K., Bernin, P., ... & Yu, S. (2002). Locus of control and well-being at work: how generalizable are western findings?. *Academy of management journal*, *45*(2), 453-466.

[24] April, K. A., Dharani, B., & Peters, K. (2012). Impact of locus of control expectancy on level of well-being. *Rev. Eur. Stud.*, *4*, 124.

likely to feel empowered and have a sense of purpose and direction. Regardless of the situation, we can typically control our communication, our actions, our attitudes, and our thoughts.

Recall that we want to try to satisfy our RISC needs—respect, identity, safety, and control—both for ourselves and the people around us. It's more likely we'll promote these needs from within our circle of control than from within our circle of concern. Even so, many of us are drawn to our circle of concern more than our circle of control. Why?

Humans are really good threat detectors. From an evolutionary perspective, we've had to be. We are more likely to survive in the world if we over-assume that things are potential threats so we can respond to them before they harm us. As such, we tend to constantly monitor our internal and external environments for danger, focusing on problems and threats rather than solutions and opportunities. This is a psychological phenomenon called negativity bias—an incredibly powerful mental heuristic that has helped keep humans alive through the ages. Yet, it has also kept us in distress.

As Peaceful Leaders, we don't want to put ourselves into a consistently distressed, negative mindset. When we do, we respond to our environments more from fear and self-interest than from patience, curiosity, and self-control. So, instead, we want to train ourselves to move from concern to control as quickly as possible and then from control to action.

Let's try it together: say you've heard about the possibility of impending layoffs. In this example, you would be worried about yourself and your team members, but you wouldn't have control over whether the layoffs are happening or who will be impacted. By definition, this situation would fall into your circle of concern.

Now, within this scenario, think of three things you *would* have control over. For example, you would have control over your quality of work, how you interact with your team members, and your communication with others about the layoffs. Take a minute and think about three more items that would fall into your circle of control.

Moving from concern to control should help you feel a bit more empowered in this situation. Now, let's move to action. Review the elements that you can control, and brainstorm three action items that you can do within your control. For example, you might choose to do extra work by taking on an additional project. Or you could choose to connect with your team members one-on-one to see how you can support them through this volatile situation. You could also choose not to perpetuate the fear of uncertainty by refusing to engage in gossip. Take a minute and think about three action items of your own.

As we move from control to action, it is important that we recognize that even inaction is a choice. But when we choose not to act from a place of control, rather than from fear or concern, we are better able to respond as Peaceful

Leaders. In other words, whether we choose to act or not to act, recognizing that we are *choosing* to do so empowers us.

To recap, our goal as patient, Peaceful Leaders is to increase our self-awareness and self-regulation when it comes to stress and emotional experiences. We can do that by stopping to create space between stress or emotion and our response, taking 10 deep breaths to promote oxygen intake and filter out the cortisol in our systems, and observing our physical sensations, thoughts, and behaviors to become more aware of our responses and reactions to the emotions; and finally proceeding from a place of patience, control, and choice rather than fear and concern.

Receiving Feedback Effectively

When employees give us feedback, we may feel defensive, angry, defeated, or resentful. This is why it's so important to learn skills that help us receive feedback patiently and effectively. When done right, receiving feedback will enhance the three pillars of Peaceful Leadership in your workplace.

When you allow people to share their voices and opinions without becoming defensive, you promote **inclusion** in your team. When you take ownership and accountability for your behavior, you increase **trust** and respect with employees. And when you model vulnerability and humility by constructively receiving feedback, you contribute to a **psychologically safe** workplace.

If, on the other hand, you don't receive or respond to feedback well, you communicate to your team that you do not take ownership or responsibility for your actions, you are not able to be vulnerable or remain open to improvement, and their voices will not be heard when they have something to say that might be hard for you to hear. As a result, your employees will have a tendency to agree with you automatically and not raise issues or ideas that may benefit the organization.

That all being said, **our goal is not to accept or adopt all feedback.** There will be feedback that we disagree with. That is okay. We don't need to agree with everything. In fact, it would be wrong to simply accept all feedback as it is given. Rather, our goal when receiving feedback is to support both the *task* and the *relationship*. We want to patiently explore and understand the feedback being given so we can better serve the work, the mission, the stakeholders, and our team members. Accordingly, we might need to depersonalize the feedback to make it not about ourselves but instead find the truth within it—even if it's misguided or poorly delivered.

If you have an impulse to react defensively to feedback, especially if it is about you or your work, try your best to use the STOP framework discussed earlier in this chapter. Become more aware of your reactions and self-regulate so you can proceed constructively. Then, adhere to the three-step process for receiving feedback outlined below.

Step 1: Listen, Repeat, and Clarify

When someone is brave enough to raise an issue or provide feedback, we start by **listening** to the feedback without responding. Give the person sharing the feedback your undivided attention so they can share what's on their mind without interruption or rebuttal.

When they are done sharing their feedback, you then **repeat** and summarize what you heard and ask any clarifying questions to ensure you fully understand the feedback. When you ask clarifying questions, try to encourage the person to be specific so you can understand their perspective as thoroughly as possible. Whatever you do, do not respond, defend or reject feedback before you confirm you understand the feedback fully. If you assume you understand without confirming, you are contributing to an environment where unnecessary conflict could occur.

Your primary goals with this step are a) to fully understand what the feedback is so you can respond accordingly, and b) to allow the person giving feedback to feel heard and understood. Oftentimes, when people give feedback, they just want to be heard. Listening without becoming defensive may take self-regulation. However, if you're able to remain humble and step outside your ego for just a few moments, you may not even need to regulate.

Step 2: Seek Hidden Gems

It doesn't matter what the feedback is about or how poorly it's delivered. You should always be on the lookout for hidden gems in someone's communication. A great place to start your search is in the answers to the following questions:

- What is the highest possible intention of this feedback?
- What is the underlying factor driving this feedback?
- If I accepted this feedback, what positive outcomes would it provide?

Nearly every piece of feedback has at least one hidden gem. But sometimes, it's not in the place you'd expect. A quick example: say your employee told you he was fed up with a project, and you know this project is one of his core duties. Initially, you might think this individual simply can't handle the work, is lazy, or just wants to complain. But upon asking clarifying questions and digging a bit further, you realize that the stress is coming not from the project itself but from a particular colleague who is constantly making things difficult. Now you've identified the actual issue: it wasn't a task-oriented problem, as was originally presented to you, but rather a relationship-oriented problem. By listening without jumping to conclusions and asking questions, you were able to find the hidden gem in the initial feedback.

Keep in mind: even if an employee is sharing feedback that doesn't have any task- or relationship-orientation value, consider the RISC needs of respect, identity, safety, and control. Perhaps the employee is not feeling satisfied at this level, and it shows through their feedback.

Step 3: Open a Dialogue

After you've patiently listened, fully understood the feedback, and found the hidden gems, it's time to open a dialogue about how to move forward whenever applicable and appropriate. When opening a dialogue, start by thanking them for feeling like they could bring the feedback to your attention, and acknowledge the hidden gems you found there. This way, you'll get the conversation started on the right foot and promote a sense of collaboration.

If you have concerns about their feedback, bring those concerns up as questions or tradeoffs rather than flat-out rejections. For example: "What you're suggesting *would* have a positive impact on overall sales. That's a great idea. I wonder if that might make some unnecessary challenges for marketing, however. Do you have any ideas on how we can support the marketing team as well?"

By offering tradeoffs and seeking more input, you're helping your employees understand your vantage point while also making them feel included and valued. Doing so builds trust and respect and helps your employees deliver more refined and complete feedback in the future.

If you do not feel it is appropriate to open a dialogue after you hear someone's feedback—perhaps you're in a bad headspace, or you simply don't have the time or space to follow the outlined steps—it's okay to not respond at that moment and redirect to a future conversation. It is completely appropriate to say, "Thank you for coming to me with this information. You've given me a lot to think about. Let me think about this and get back to you by tomorrow." Or: "I want to hear more about what you have to say when we have more time to connect. Let's schedule a time to talk later this week. How's Thursday at 2 pm?"

When you schedule a later time to reconnect about the feedback, make sure you do so in a timely manner. Don't leave it open-ended and then fail to follow up.

Remember, the core competency of patience is all about staying in control of your emotions, your communications, and your actions. We tend to be the most reactive when we're receiving feedback. This week, be on the lookout for instances where you are being given feedback and how you respond. If you pay close attention, you may find that people are offering feedback more often than you realize. Find an opportunity where someone is offering you feedback and practice patience by listening, seeking understanding, finding the hidden gems, and engaging in a solution-focused dialogue.

Case Narrative:

From our perspective, Connor had to enhance his patience around relationship-awareness and relationship-navigation. We performed a RISC analysis to more clearly understand the contributing factors:

Respect: Was Renee feeling unseen, unheard, and unappreciated for her contributions? Was Connor? Did either lack care and attention? Through our discovery, it was clear that both Connor and Renee felt misunderstood and disrespected.

Identity: Did either feel that a part of their identity was harmed? Either with regard to their specific role and responsibilities or a larger aspect of their identity? Through gathering more information, it was determined that Renee was interpreting Connor's implementation of particular policies as digs on her identity as a woman.

Safety: What was the comfort level in speaking up? Was there fear of negative repercussions? Renee certainly felt a lack of psychological safety, considering Connor's failure to recognize or ask her about reasonable accommodations for her personal issues.

Control: Did either Connor or Renee feel as though they had no control over the situation? Was a lack of control contributing to their distress? Renee's perception of Connor taking control and overpowering her resulted in her feeling less control over her life. While she did her due diligence in communicating with HR for her accommodations, the action of the write-up triggered her distress. As things progressed, Connor also began to feel a lack of control, as he was increasingly confused about how to lead Renee appropriately, how to communicate with her without triggering her, and how to hold her accountable without coming off as a brute.

The distress at play between Connor and Renee stems from the real or perceived threat to their underlying needs of Respect, Identity, Safety, and Control. These needs were not satisfied, leading both of them to commit the common cognitive errors referenced earlier in the chapter, reinforcing the interpretations and stories they told themselves.

Once we facilitated dialogues between the two, they began to become aware of this social-psychological dynamic. Hearing how each of their fundamental needs were being affected opened their eyes to how one another's words and actions were affecting each other and themselves. We then worked on methods of self-analysis (i.e., practicing a RISC analysis on oneself) and ways of calmly requesting support from each other when a need gets depleted.

For example, Renee might say, "Connor, I'm feeling a bit frustrated. Yesterday morning was very difficult for me, and I needed a bit more personal time. When I asked you for a longer break, however, you were very short with me, and that felt like you were angry with me. Were you angry, or did I just misinterpret? In the future, when I need some time, what would be a better way of asking so you don't get frustrated, too?"

And Connor might say, "Sometimes, when I'm busy, I'm not quite thinking about how my demeanor affects others. I might be very short, but it's usually because I'm feeling so busy or overwhelmed. It doesn't have anything to do with you. I start getting frustrated when you tell me I'm being mean or angry, but really, I'm just overwhelmed. So, maybe there's a better way for me to make sure you know it's not about you. Any suggestions?"

During the intervention, we worked with each of them to write out feedback statements like this, making requests for their needs, then practicing with each other so they felt increasingly comfortable remaining patient while giving and receiving feedback and asking for support.

STRATEGY SESSION

Okay, let's see how you can be more patient with your team. See if you can finish the following sentences.

I would be a more patient leader if I......

If I did that, I would be more effective as a leader because......

A challenge for me to grow in this area is.....

To overcome this challenge, I can......

My first step to being a more patient leader is......

CHAPTER 6

Engagement

Engagement is a broad term—it could mean just about anything, and it doesn't always imply constructive engagement. Seeing as engagement is our second core competency; we don't want to promote engagement simply for the sake of being engaged. We want you to start thinking about how to engage with your team, specifically as a Peaceful Leader.

In this context, engagement denotes one's ability to elicit the full participation of others on the team. One study[25] found that 59% of the variance in leader effectiveness can be explained by "the leader's ability to motivate others, communicate effectively, and build teams." When combined, these qualities can be considered tantamount to a leader's capacity for engaging team members. While it may seem

---

[25] Gilley, A., McMillan, H. S., & Gilley, J. W. (2009). Organizational change and characteristics of leadership effectiveness. *Journal of Leadership & Organizational Studies, 16(1),* 38-47.

obvious, many studies have shown that engaging employees helps lead to all kinds of positive outcomes, such as fulfillment of employee needs, job satisfaction, employee well-being, individual performance, and organizational performance.[26]

Through our peacebuilding work, we've identified a handful of fundamental skills leaders can employ to boost engagement—and cultivate a working environment that promotes the three pillars of psychological safety, employee trust, and inclusion. As you move through this chapter, you'll learn how to align your team with the organization's mission, supporting people to work toward a shared goal and common purpose. You'll also discover essential tools to coach your employees through professional challenges.

Aligning the Team with the Company's Mission

In their book *Built to Last: Successful Habits of Visionary Companies,* authors Jim Collins and Jerry Porras write: "Building a visionary company is 1% Vision and 99% Alignment." Aligning your team to the company's mission means individual employees understand and can clearly communicate how their work advances the team's goals and

---

[26] Sun, L., & Bunchapattanasakda, C. (2019). Employee engagement: A literature review. *International Journal of Human Resource Studies*, 9(1), 63-80.

objectives, as well as how the *team's* work advances the *company's* mission. Achieving alignment helps employees rally around a collective purpose in their work, motivating and engaging them and contributing to their sense of **psychological safety, inclusion,** and belonging within the group; it also helps employees gain clarity about their role, which contributes to predictability and **trust** in you, as a leader, and the organization, as a whole.

By contrast, misalignment and a lack of clarity with regard to one's priorities, direction, or role are common causes of conflict and a surefire way to disengage employees. To illustrate this, imagine the following dynamic in a private healthcare office. The doctors believe the organization's mission is to offer high-quality holistic care to their patients, which translates to long and thorough appointments. However, the scheduling staff believes their mission is to treat as many members of the community as possible, which translates to brief, efficient appointments. Even though both groups are serving a worthwhile mission, they are not working in alignment. This is likely to cause conflict between the doctors and the schedulers because their actions are actively undermining and working against each other. It is also likely that schedulers would feel less motivated since they are not clear on how their work is supposed to advance the mission.

To help you more closely align your team with the company's mission—and increase engagement in the process—we've created the following four-step process.

Step 1: Define the Company's Mission

Before you can expect your team to articulate the mission of your organization, you should be clear about what it looks and feels like when your organization is living out its mission. Once you have a clear definition of your mission, educate your team and organization to help them understand what outcomes they should expect to see as your mission is being advanced. What kind of work should be taking place? What would you hear from your stakeholders? What KPIs or measurement criteria would you see?

One way to do this is to facilitate a dialogue at your next company retreat or all-team meeting, bringing teams together to discuss what it would look like for the organization to live out its mission. An exercise like this can help cross-functional units understand how one another sees the company's mission and move forward in closer alignment.

When it comes to the aforementioned private healthcare office, the organization should clarify whether it wants employees to work toward high-quality holistic care or treat the broader community. If it wants to do both, leadership needs to have a clear understanding of what that means in practice and how different teams within the organization can work together to advance this mission. Before making any firm decision in your own organization, you may want to engage key members of your staff, thereby making the development of your mission an inclusive process.

Step 2: Communicate the Company's Mission

Once the mission is clear, how will you articulate and circulate it so that everyone is on the same page? Firstly, if you do not already have one, you may want to consider coming up with a company slogan or mission statement that can be included in company communication, email signatures, company brochures, or newsletters. Neither employees nor the general public should have to search too hard to clearly understand the company's mission.

Additionally, reinforcing the company mission and mission-oriented actions throughout the year can be important. You might do this at weekly team meetings, at annual company retreats, or at any other events that seem appropriate.

Step 3: Create Clear Roles and Responsibilities

When employees have different expectations for who is responsible for what, the environment is ripe for disengagement and conflict. To avoid creating this kind of environment, it's critical you make sure your team members clearly understand their roles and responsibilities, as well as how their individual contributions support the organization's mission.

If you haven't done so already, it may be wise to include the details of an individual's responsibilities in employee job descriptions. You may even want to create an abbreviated version of these descriptions and share them with your team, so employees not only understand their own roles but also the roles of their colleagues. As roles and responsibilities shift, you'll need to regularly review and update these descriptions accordingly in order to ensure everyone is aligned.

If you're just getting started on clearly defining roles or haven't addressed the topic in a while, you can try asking your employees themselves how they view their respective roles and responsibilities that contribute to the organization's mission. Their responses can help you understand what your team thinks they should be doing (and the extent to which their perception differs from your own); it will also create an opportunity to engage them in the process of creating alignment within the team. Doing this on an annual basis allows you to address any confusion before conflicts have the chance to fester. You may also want to implement a company-wide or team-wide initiative for each team member to review their own job description, update it as necessary, and send it to their direct supervisor for final approval each year.

Step 4: Regularly Acknowledge Impact

Routinely engaging with your team to help them see the connection between their daily work and the impact it has on the organization's mission does two important things. First, it serves as a consistent reminder of the organization's mission. Sometimes we get so caught up in the minutia of our day-to-day grind that it's easy to lose sight of the big picture; these reminders encourage individuals to get out of their silos and see their work from the perspective of their team or the organization as a whole, which can strengthen feelings of psychological safety and inclusion.

The second thing that regularly acknowledging employees' impact does is promote a sense of purpose and meaning, even in seemingly small tasks and activities. Organizational psychologist Adam Grant has said that "motivation depends on balancing what's meaningful with what's manageable." Meaningfulness in work is incredibly important for keeping employees engaged. Thinking back to our scenario at the private healthcare office, it's quite possible scheduling appointments day after day could become mundane after a few years. However, if leaders of the organization frequently help the scheduler see their job as contributing to an important mission, they're likely to feel more motivated to do their jobs. They're also likely to feel more satisfied at work (and therefore less likely to quit).

One way to do this might be to share client success stories with the whole team so everyone can see the impact their collective action is having. You might also consider sending out weekly emails to your team, connecting specific work activities for that week to the company's mission. Or incorporate these acknowledgments into your regular team meetings so everyone can recognize the impact of individual contributions. If you're going to engage in "public" recognition of your team members, do your best to recognize everyone at some point for what they are bringing to the table (i.e., if some get recognized regularly and others rarely do, this may cause conflict).

In sum, outlining a mission statement only to let it gather dust on the proverbial shelf doesn't help anyone. Bring your organization's mission to life and anchor alignment into your culture by frequently and meaningfully engaging with your team. As you continue through this chapter, consider the four-step process and try to think of some small but significant ways to more closely align your team with the organization's mission.

Coaching Employees: What It Is and Why It's Important

Coaching is a highly supportive and engaging approach that allows team members to *explore* ideas and *own* their actions. Whereas many leaders are accustomed to simply assigning responsibilities, delegating work tasks, making decisions, or giving directions, a Peaceful Leader strives to implement a coaching mindset. Ultimately, this will encourage team members to be responsible for exploring their own options, making their own decisions, and shaping their own professional growth, all of which promote engagement in work life.

Imagine this: Late in the afternoon, a team member comes into your office with a problem they need help with. It's a pretty routine problem; maybe you've even addressed it several times before. Naturally, it would be easy for you to simply tell your employee how to handle the situation so you can get back to work.

In this situation, our response is often a directive—we know the solution or pathway forward and delegate an employee to execute it. Yet, if all a leader does is direct and delegate to their team, over time, employees will become overly reliant on them for guidance and will ultimately disengage from their work.

What if we instead choose to put our work aside and engage in a coaching conversation with the team member? Perhaps we say, "Thanks for bringing this to my attention. Let's talk this through. What are your initial thoughts on how to handle this?" Depending on their response, you might follow up by asking: "If you did that, would it solve the issue?" Or: "Are there any other issues this might create in the process?"

These are just a few examples. But you can see how coaching can become a key tool in a Peaceful Leader's arsenal. When we take a few minutes to coach a team member toward finding their own answers—as opposed to offering a clear solution ourselves—we help them build awareness of how to resolve the situation themselves. Not only does coaching help them explore and evaluate the different options at play, but it also helps them get into the habit of thinking through and resolving similar issues in the future.

When you decide to engage with your team through a coaching approach, you can always bring your own experience and insight to bear on the exploration, using particular questions to nudge the employee in the right direction. And if it's not working, you may then reverse course to direct and delegate. But by defaulting to coaching first, you get to know how your team thinks and approaches their work, which will help you build trust in their capacities and learn how best to support them in their professional growth. Additionally, you set the expectation that when they come to you with an issue, they will have a voice in creating a possible solution. Over time, they will learn to come to you only *after they've thought the problem through themselves.* As they continue to refine their approach to various difficult situations, the coaching conversations will become more sophisticated. In effect, you'll be slowly helping them become leaders themselves.

Coaching as a Peaceful Leader requires an investment of time and energy in the short term, but it will likely pay off in the long run as team members grow more autonomous and effective in their roles. Eventually, your team will feel like you **trust** them to make decisions, reinforcing their trust in you.

They'll feel included because they'll have a voice in decision-making, especially when the decisions impact their work. And finally, they'll feel more respected, valued, and, therefore, psychologically safe in their working environment.

Now, let's go over some practical and easy-to-use techniques to engage your team in coaching conversations.

Coaching Employees: Practical Techniques

First things first: when we adopt a coaching mindset as a Peaceful Leader, we want to take a **high support** and **high challenge** approach. By high support, we mean a leader's ability to provide a safe environment for their team to openly explore solutions to issues, in which they know the leader has their back. By high challenge, we mean a leader's ability to encourage their team to take different perspectives, get out of their comfort zone, and grow as people and professionals.

What happens if we don't offer a high-support, high-challenge approach? If we offer **low support** and **low challenge**, we'll likely spread indifference throughout our team. People will lose interest and be less motivated and more likely to disengage. If we offer **low support** and **high challenge**, we'll likely create a high-stress work environment, fostering burnout, resentment, and higher turnover. If we offer **high support** and **low challenge**, our team might feel bored, and their growth may plateau since they're able to stay in their comfort zone.

When we offer **high support** and **high challenge**, we promote a **growth** zone for our team. There may be times when you variably need to boost your level of support or challenge. However, your goal as a coach should be to offer support and challenge in equal measure so your team can grow in their roles and professions.

Here are three key coaching skills you can start developing and incorporating into a high-support and high-challenge approach right away.

Skill #1: Attentional Listening

Attentional listening is our ability to listen completely, with our full *attention* focused on the person we're coaching. We are capable of thinking much faster than we speak. So, while someone else is talking to us, we often have plenty of mental space to let our minds wander. Maybe you have a deadline coming up, or you're having issues at home, or you just remembered you need to add something to your grocery list. If you're thinking about these things while listening to someone speak, you're not giving them your full attention. In addition to thinking about other tasks or problems while listening, we also have thoughts, judgments, and biases about the individual talking to us and what they're saying. These judgments diminish our attention as well.

When we're in a coaching mindset, we have to make sure we're giving the individual we're supporting our full, undivided attention. We need to put in the effort to focus on the person, eliminate mind-wandering, and let go of judgment. To aid with this, try employing reflective listening—a technique that requires active listening for the purpose of repeating back or paraphrasing what you just heard from someone. Listening and repeating is incredibly validating for the person you are listening to and will help you actively focus on what they're saying.

Our full, non-judgmental attention enables us to be better at using our other coaching skills and allows us, as leaders, to stay curious and supportive, creating an atmosphere where team members feel comfortable speaking up. Within this environment, employees feel more engaged with the task and the organization.

Skill #2: Ask, Don't Tell

Remember: When it comes to coaching, we're trying to move away from directing and delegating and toward inquiry and asking questions in order to help our team members explore the situation or issue for themselves and find a solution that works for them.

The most powerful forms of questions come from genuine curiosity. As you're developing a coaching mind, try centering your inquiry around a **high-ask**, **low-tell** framework. In other words, do your best to ask a lot of questions that help lead others to their own answers rather than tell people what to do or lead them to *your* answers. This approach to coaching helps develop people's problem-solving capabilities and allows them to identify realistic pathways forward that are going to work for them.

You might begin with statements like, "I would be curious to know…" or "Tell me more about…" When you open with one of these two phrases, you're opening space for collaboration, curiosity, and dialogue. As you become more comfortable with asking questions in coaching situations, you may want to try more advanced methods of inquiry, such as time-based inquiry, perspective-based inquiry, and specificity inquiry.

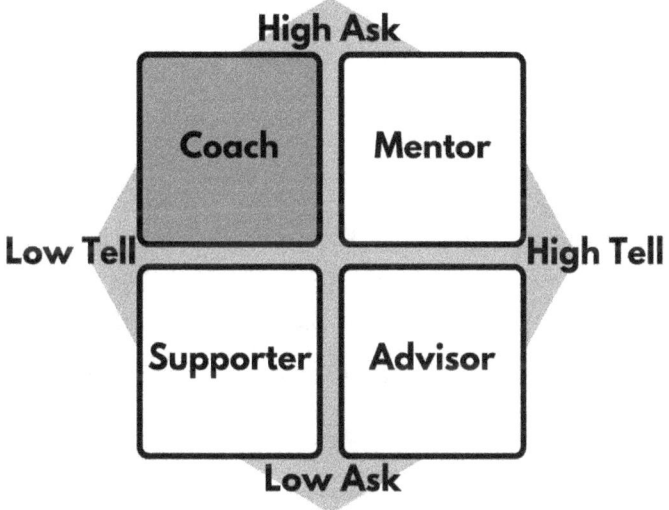

Time-Based Inquiry

When we are faced with a challenge, it is easy to get stuck focusing on only one element of time. We may be stuck in the past, ruminating about what *has* happened. We also may get stuck in the present, blocked from moving forward because of the pressure or stress of what *is* happening. Or we may get stuck in the future, concerned about what *will* happen. Time-based inquiry is meant to help someone get out of their stuck state and explore the situation from different time-based perspectives.

Let's say Mary has had a conflict with one of her colleagues for the past few weeks. They have different approaches to completing shared projects, which impacts their working relationship, their shared projects, and their teams. Mary is stressed and overwhelmed by the situation and is stuck in the present moment, feeling paralyzed about how to move forward.

Here are a few ways that we can help Mary explore the situation through time-based inquiry:

Bring the future to the present...
"*What would you like to be saying about this a year from now?*"

Helping Mary consider the big picture of the situation by imagining a future world where this problem is resolved might give her a template for what she wants out of the situation. Visiting the future and then returning to the present can often help employees in a stuck state expand their thinking to what is possible and what they are willing to do to reach that future possibility.

Bring the past to the present.
"*What did you do the last time something like this happened?*"

Bringing the past to the present can elicit resourcefulness. A question like this might help Mary think through past challenges collaborating with colleagues. The strategies she used in those situations might apply to the present situation.

Bring the present to the future.
"*If you did _____, what would be your first step?*"
"*If you did _____, how would it bring you closer to your goals?*"

Let's assume Mary came up with an idea while exploring past situations. Once she has an option for resolution, you might want to help her explore what the future would look like if she moved forward with that strategy and whether the strategy would help move her toward her future goals.

Perspective-Based Inquiry

Similar to being stuck in a timeframe, it is also natural to become stuck in our own perspective on the situation. Imagine a challenging situation you were in recently that caused you stress or anxiety. As you are reflecting on that situation, whose perspective are you reflecting on? We would feel confident predicting that you are reflecting from your perspective rather than someone else's. This is because it is challenging to dissociate from our own perspective, especially when it causes a heightened emotional experience.

When coaching someone, it can be helpful to ask questions to promote dissociation from the situation to broaden their perspective. Let's jump back in and see how we might use perspective-based inquiry to support Mary's situation with her colleague.

Bring other perspectives to Mary.
"If you were to ask me for advice, what advice do you think I would give you?"
"What would your team members, who are being impacted by the situation, say if they were involved in this conversation?"

By considering other perspectives on the situation, Mary can start to get a more complete and unbiased vantage point. Promoting a dissociated perspective can encourage Mary to approach the situation with a bit more of a rational mindset rather than an emotionally charged state.

Bring Mary's perspective to her colleagues.
"What doesn't your colleague understand about your perspective?"
"How might you help them understand it?"

Helping Mary explore her perspective through her colleague's lens might help her clarify why she feels stuck in the dynamic. It also might help her consider what she needs to do or communicate with her colleague to reach a resolution.

Specificity Inquiry

When we get stuck in a situation, we often lean on mental shortcuts or labels to explain the situation or our goals. As a coach, it is essential that we help our employees get really clear on what they want out of the situation. This way, we know what the goal is, and they can better communicate that goal to others when appropriate.

The specificity inquiry is a great tool when your team uses abstract, vague language to describe a situation or desired outcomes. Let's check back in with Mary and see how we can use this to support her.

<u>Breakdown labels and create clear goals</u>
"You say you want to be successful on this project with your colleague. What does success look like to you?"

Success is a label that Mary is using to describe what she wants from the situation abstractly. Her colleagues might want success, too, but if they aren't clear on what success means to them, reaching alignment on a solution will be challenging. From a coaching perspective, we want to help Mary clarify what specific actions, behaviors, communications, project outcomes, etc. she will see when she and her colleague are successful, which will help her communicate to her colleague about what she needs.

Identify specific interests and values.
"What is important to you about being successful with your colleague?"

By understanding what is driving her "success" goal, Mary will have more clarity on why it is important to her. Mary may have many interests that drive her toward wanting success. For the sake of this example, let's say her main interest is to promote a positive work environment for her team. Understanding her WHY helps prepare her to brainstorm options on how to move forward to manifest a positive work environment for her team, not necessarily only on how to be successful with her colleagues. This is a great tool to expand possibilities and increase the level of control Mary has over the situation.

Coaching your team members using inquiry allows them to think through situations and issues to identify more complete and durable options for resolution. It also helps your team develop a problem-solving mindset that will lead them to seek less support or, at the very least, come to you for support after having already analyzed the situation. Coaching can take some time investment, but you are investing in your team members to be more independent and effective in their roles.

Skill #3: The Map App

One easy way to structure your coaching process is through the paradigm of an app many of us use regularly. When you're lost and trying to find your way, you might pull out your phone and open a map application. When we're lost at work or can't find our way in a new situation or issue, a Peaceful Leader can offer similar support.

Just like in a map app, a leader should help their team member identify their **current location** and their **desired destination**. Even if they don't quite know how to get there yet, their clearer understanding of where they're starting from and where they're going can provide a solid foundation for confidently devising the next steps.

To help them out, you might ask your employee simple questions like, "What specifically is the challenge you feel like you're facing right now?" or "How are you hoping this issue will be resolved?"

Once you've set your current location and desired destination, a map app will give you different **routes** to evaluate and choose from. As a coach, you can give your employees the equivalent by asking them questions such as: "What options do you have?" and "What are the pros and cons of each of those options?" Sometimes, it can be helpful to encourage the person you're coaching to come up with at least three "routes" before choosing how to move forward;

that way, they don't simply jump at the first possibility, which may not be the best option.

A map app can also **reroute** you if you're heading in the wrong direction. As a coach, rerouting can sound like: "What will you do if you get off track?" or "What will you do if something unexpected happens?" These types of questions can help you ensure your employee is resilient and resourceful when unexpected obstacles inevitably appear on the way to their desired destination.

Lastly, a map app will tell you when you are getting close to and have **arrived** at your destination. As a coach, it's our job to help our team members identify when they've been successful. You might ask, "How will you know you are making progress as you move forward?" or "What behaviors or actions will you see when this issue is resolved?" Knowing the answers to these questions ahead of time will give team members a sense of accomplishment when they finally reach their destination. These questions also reinforce hard work, dedication, and professional growth—the more people feel as though they're making progress toward goals at work, the more likely they are to stay highly engaged.

This week, try to find opportunities to use some of the skills and techniques covered in this chapter to help one of your team members move through a tricky situation or see how their contributions are furthering the organization's mission. This may take time and energy on your part, but keep in mind that you're making an investment in the development of your team members and their abilities to be more independent and efficient. As a result of this investment, you'll cultivate a workplace where employees can trust you, feel safe to ask for help when they need it, and are included in both goal-setting and action plans for achieving those goals.

Case Narrative: Engagement

When Connor received his promotion, he assumed his new role and responsibilities with enthusiasm. Again, he thought of himself less as a mentor and more as a colleague, which he felt was the right mindset for a manager. However, he did not realize that with leadership, he could contribute to his team members' feelings of value and engagement by being a mentor or coach. In fact, the idea of coaching others seemed not only foreign but, in some ways, pretentious to Connor. Who was he to coach others? This was an interesting aspect we learned about Connor during the Peacemaking process: he hadn't fully bought into his own value in this new role.

Therefore, we helped him learn new techniques to engage and coach others that would allow him to feel even more valuable as a leader. Not only was he technically good at his job, leading to his promotion, he also had a ton of potential in inspiring and engaging team members, which would be a large part of his new role.

For example, when Renee brought Connor an issue regarding her inability to be at the upcoming all-team meeting, his natural inclination was to become frustrated, dismissive, and directive. Instead, we challenged him to engage Renee from a place of care and to use coaching techniques to help her arrive at her own answers. *"So, it sounds like you're going to have trouble meeting your personal obligations if you attend the meeting this week. I understand. Are you up for a little brainstorming here? Great! Is there anyone that could help take care of some of the personal stuff? Is there any way to get that done right after the meeting or on a different day? If you have to miss the meeting, what would be the best way to get the information we went over? How can I support you better in making sure you meet your obligations?"*

By attending to Renee's needs and engaging her with powerful questions rather than telling her what to do, Connor helped Renee come to a solution that she could really buy into. Additionally, this attentive questioning helped Renee build more trust—that she could come to Connor with an issue, and he would actually help rather than dismiss her or become annoyed. The increasing trust with her manager was helping her feel more engaged at work, which ultimately led to her missing less work and fewer meetings. A Win for all.

STRATEGY SESSION

Okay, let's see how you can be more engaging with your team. See if you can finish the following sentences.

I would be a more engaging leader if I......

If I did that, I would be more effective as a leader because......

A challenge for me to grow in this area is.....

To overcome this challenge, I can......

My first step to being a more engaging leader is......

CHAPTER 7

Appreciation

Within the field of positive psychology, the concept of gratitude—or **appreciation**—has been highlighted not only as a personal trait associated with well-being[27] but also as a "vital civic virtue."[28] Leaders who exhibit appreciative behaviors—e.g., publicly or privately recognizing good performance—help employees feel more supported[29] and understood, which is positively tied to performance.[30] These

---

[27] Wood, A. M., Froh, J. J., & Geraghty, A. W. (2010). Gratitude and well-being: A review and theoretical integration. *Clinical Psychology Review, 30(7),* 890-905.

[28] Emmons, R. A., & Shelton, C. M. (2002). Gratitude and the science of positive psychology. *Handbook of positive psychology, 18,* 463.

[29] Amabile, T. M., Schatzel, E. A., Moneta, G. B., & Kramer, S. J. (2004). Leader behaviors and the work environment for creativity: Perceived leader support. *The Leadership Quarterly, 15(1),* 5-32.

[30] Shao, P., Graham, K. A., Zhou, Z., Li, H., & Zhao, L. (2021). You make me feel understood and trusted: The role of leader appreciation expression. In Academy of Management Proceedings (Vol. 2021, No. 1, p. 11721). Briarcliff Manor, NY 10510: Academy of Management.

behaviors can also lead to team members being more willing to speak up and be innovative.[31] Moreover, when individuals are thanked, they experience boosts in self-efficacy and prosocial behavior.[32]

Intuitively, you probably have a pretty good idea of how to show your appreciation. But are you doing so in a way that enhances the three pillars of Peaceful Leadership? In this context, appreciation is so much more than simply telling someone you appreciate them. To be effective, it is a skill that requires cultivation and practice.

Through our work as Peacebuilders, we've identified a few essential skills related to appreciation that every Peaceful Leader should be able to use in the workplace. In this chapter, you'll learn how to cultivate a strength-based mindset and implement a strength-based approach in your leadership. We will also present a framework for facilitating employee reviews in a way that promotes safety, trust, and inclusion.

---

[31] Li, C., Dong, Y., Wu, C. H., Brown, M. E., & Sun, L. Y. (2021). Appreciation that inspires: The impact of leader trait gratitude on team innovation. *Journal of Organizational Behavior*.

[32] Grant, A. M., & Gino, F. (2010). A little thanks goes a long way: Explaining why gratitude expressions motivate prosocial behavior. *Journal of Personality and Social Psychology, 98(6)*, 946–955.

Developing a Strength-Based Mindset

A **strength-based mindset** is one in which we focus on opportunities and strengths rather than on problems or weaknesses. The opposite of a strength-based mindset is a deficit-based mindset— a type of thinking that focuses on the problems, rather than the possibilities.

3 key assumptions of a <u>Strength-based mindset</u>.

1. **There is always something that works.**
2. **Our thoughts reinforce themselves.**
3. **Our language helps frame our reality.**

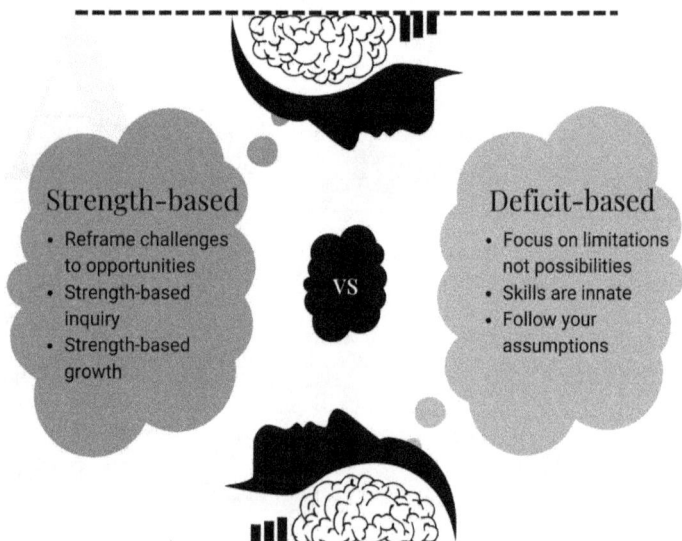

Strength–based

- Reframe challenges to opportunities
- Strength-based inquiry
- Strength-based growth

VS

Deficit–based

- Focus on limitations not possibilities
- Skills are innate
- Follow your assumptions

When we operate from a strength-based mindset at work, we lay the foundation for employees to feel valued and supported, which cultivates psychological safety, employee trust, and inclusion. It also allows us to deliver challenging feedback without losing our employees' trust or respect because we are focusing on the development of their strengths—as opposed to the limitations of their weaknesses—and coming from a place of care. (Indeed, research has shown that deploying this approach when giving feedback leads to higher employee engagement, well-being, and productivity.[33])

Adopting a strength-based mindset is key for any Peaceful Leader looking to become fluent in the core competency of appreciation. But to do so, you must first be willing to make some fundamental assumptions about human nature.

Fundamental Assumption #1: Within Every Weakness, There's an Undiscovered Strength

We all have strengths and weaknesses. No matter how many flaws we each have, there are always areas in which we exhibit excellence. As leaders, we must be willing to focus on others' strengths in order to help them grow. In addition, we must also be willing to seek out and surface the underlying

---

[33] Aguinis, H., Gottfredson, R. K., & Joo, H. (2012). Delivering effective performance feedback: The strengths-based approach. *Business Horizons*, 55(2), 105-111.

strengths that may be hiding in perceived weaknesses or undesirable behaviors.

Let's say David has a history of poor communication with his colleagues. He tends to be long-winded and sometimes raises his voice to others in the workplace. People routinely refer to him as aggressive and hot-tempered. As a leader or manager, it's easy to look at David and see only his flaws and areas for improvement. But let's consider how this perceived weakness could actually stand to serve David, his team, and the organization.

It's evident from his communication style that David is a passionate individual who loves his work. He prides himself on going to bat for his team and clients. David tends to get whatever job he wants because his passion separates him from other applicants; typically, he receives glowing reviews from his clients. While it's clearly one of his most valuable assets, David's passion can also end up harming the team.

Let's reframe how we look at David's behaviors. Instead of only seeing the issues that we need to address, let's practice recognizing and appreciating the strengths underneath those behaviors and support him in refining tools he can use more constructively. We can work with David on how to use his passionate energy in more productive ways and how to recognize when he is a bit too overzealous.

The first step toward developing a strength-based mindset is to start appreciating and building on your employees' strengths, which means we need to be committed to *discovering* them. With David, it's crucial to identify the strength lurking within an ostensibly undesirable behavior—and to work with him on channeling his passion in more productive ways.

Fundamental Assumption #2: Our thoughts reinforce themselves

To develop a strength-based mindset, it is important to recognize that, like habits, we form patterns in our thought processes that reinforce a particular way of thinking.

If we look at David and all we see are his flaws and weaknesses, we are creating a pattern of thinking that reinforces a deficit-based mindset, which will make it more difficult for us to spot examples of his strengths in the future. On the other hand, when we focus on strengths and opportunities for growth, we direct our thoughts toward someone's potential rather than their limitations, and we develop a pattern of thinking that makes it easier for us to see the strengths people have to offer.

These patterns dictate what we tend to pay attention to and what we tend to ignore, which influences our actions, behaviors, and communication with others. If we adopt a deficit-based mindset, we might label David as a problem or a liability. From this vantage point, it might seem reasonable to respond by trying to correct his behaviors. But if we adopt a strength-based mindset, we might label David as a developing professional or a company asset in need of a bit of guidance. This reframing encourages us to approach the situation with appreciation, curiosity, and a commitment to growth.

Every thought we have reinforces or changes our worldview. As such, changing our thought patterns, and thus how we perceive the world, is one of the hardest things we can do. Try taking inventory of your thoughts about the people around you and ask yourself: are you operating within a deficit-based mindset or a strength-based mindset? For an exercise, see the three-step process on assumption number three at the end of the next section.

Fundamental Assumption #3: Our language helps construct our reality

Not only do our thoughts reinforce themselves—they also inform our language. In turn, the language we use helps construct our reality.

Language:
- Helps us describe and define our world.
- Helps others understand how *we* view the world.
- It can even influence how *others* view the world.

When we respond from a deficit-based mindset, the language we use to describe our perceptions may prompt others to adopt a deficit-based mindset as well.

We all can relate to this. When someone tells you that you did a good job, the feedback suggests others view you as a valuable contributor to the team, increasing the likelihood that you feel appreciated and effective in your role. But if someone tells you that you did a bad job, you might feel like your efforts and contributions don't matter, increasing the likelihood that you feel unappreciated or inadequate.

The emotions we experience with positive feedback and negative feedback are vastly different. In fact, we are much more likely to be impacted by negative feedback than positive feedback, and the impact of negative feedback typically stays with us for much longer than the impact of positive feedback[34]. When we receive positive feedback, most of us experience it fleetingly—it may offer a boost of positivity that quickly subsides as we move on to other tasks throughout our day. However, negative feedback tends to impact us for a much longer duration and with greater emotional salience— it can feel crushing and linger for days, weeks, or even months after the experience.

Research has indicated that the higher ratio of positive, strength-based language to negative, deficit-based language contributes to a higher-performing team.[35] This research suggests that having a ratio of 6:1 positive to negative language from leaders in the workplace increases the

[34] Baumeister, R. F., Bratslavsky, E., Finkenauer, C., & Vohs, K. D. (2001). Bad is stronger than good. *Review of general psychology*, 5(4), 323-370.

[35] Zenger, J., & Folkman, J. (2013). The ideal praise-to-criticism ratio. *Harvard Business Review, 15.*

development of a strength-based mindset within the organization and enhances team performance.

So, if you're interested in viewing your team through a strength-based framework, which will ultimately influence how you give feedback, try following these three steps.

Step 1: Reflect

Reflect on your thoughts about the people around you. Consider whether your thoughts are typically deficit-based, focusing on what people lack, or strength-based, emphasizing their positive qualities and abilities. Recognizing and acknowledging your thought patterns is the first step toward changing them.

Step 2: Reframe

Once you have identified an area where you have a deficit-based mindset, reframe your thoughts to focus on strengths instead. Find something positive about the person, behavior, or situation. Consider thinking about how the deficit you are noticing might be benefiting other people, the team, the organization, or even yourself. Incorporate the strengths you identify into your perspective on the situation and your approach when responding.

Step 3: Reinforce

Continuously reinforce your strength-based mindset by focusing on and highlighting the strengths of those around you, including your own. Acknowledge and verbalize strengths, successes, and accomplishments, especially when there are many deficits to overcome. Over time, a strength-based mindset will become second nature, leading to improved relationships and higher performance.

Implementing a Strength-Based Mindset

Adopting a strength-based mindset with our star employees, or when everything is going well, comes naturally. But how do we adopt a strength-based mindset when it's more challenging to see the strengths in others? What follows are a few tools for implementing a strengths-based approach, even with more difficult employees.

Tool #1: Framing and Reframing

Our goal with reframing is to help others see and appreciate their own strengths and value as foundations for growth and development. Reframing how we communicate about issues, problems, or weaknesses should be done in a three-step process:

1. **Reframe the issue, problem, or weaknesses to *ourselves*.** In the previous section, we discussed the example of David's problem communicating with his team. Initially, we would likely perceive this behavior as undesirable. But we can reframe the behavior to ourselves by identifying its underlying value, strength, and/or positive contribution. Perhaps we reframe "David's problem

communicating" as David "being very passionate about his work."

2. **Make sure your reframing will not cause harm to others.** For instance, if David insulted a co-worker in a fit of passion, we wouldn't want to reframe that behavior because it would feel minimizing or dismissive to the person David harmed.

3. **Communicate the reframed perspective to set up an opportunity for growth.** We might say to David: "David, I love the passion and energy you bring into your work. Though, I've noticed that your energy has not been received well by your team lately. I don't want you to lose the passion you have for your work, and I also want your team to feel excited about working with you. Can we work together to find a way of optimizing both?"

Here are a few other examples of reframing a perceived behavioral problem to accentuate its underlying value:

The perceived behavioral problem: Not coordinating with others before taking action.

The reframe: Fearlessness, self-confidence, being a go-getter.

The perceived behavioral problem: Being distrustful of others.

The reframe: Being careful, cautious, and protective.

The perceived behavioral problem: Impulsiveness.

The reframe: Quick-thinking and decisive.

The perceived behavioral problem: Being long-winded or over-communicative.

The reframe: Being a complex thinker.

Tool #2: Strength-Based Inquiry

The goal of strength-based inquiry is to ask questions that help the individual highlight and explore their strengths so they can be more intentional about employing those attributes in all areas of their work. By inquiring from a strength-based mindset or asking questions that elicit strength-based thinking, we can encourage people to see, explore, and appreciate their own strengths in addition to the value they bring to the team and organization.

In the previous section, we reframed David's poor communication as a passion for his work, which has served him well in the past. As a next step, a strength-based inquiry would help us determine whether he can use his passion for work to develop stronger relationships with his team.

We might start with a question that allows David to see how his passion has helped him in similar situations. For example: "Can you think of a time when your passion for the job helped strengthen your relationships around the office?"

We might then prompt him to consider why it worked in the past. "How did it strengthen your relationships? What did you do specifically? What were some other contributing factors?"

We could even go further then and ask him how he might achieve a similar result in the present: "How could you bring those contributing factors into your work with your current team?"

Tool #3: Building from the Strengths Up

Now that we have successfully reframed the issues and behaviors to find the underlying value, and we have inquired from a strength-based mindset to explore how an employee's strengths have worked in the past, we can start to help someone build on their strengths and address their weaknesses. When addressing weaknesses from a strength-based mindset, it's important to make your team members feel supported, even as you're focusing on areas of improvement. Here are three solid ways to do that:

1. **Address weaknesses from an information and skill perspective, not an innate talent perspective**. Information and skills can be acquired and learned, indicating the potential to learn and grow. An innate talent perspective implies that there are limits to what can be taught, which communicates to your team members that you believe they are simply weak in a certain area and there isn't much they can do about it. In David's example, this would be the difference between framing his challenge as a

communication skill that can be improved rather than an innate personality trait that cannot be.

2. Put in place **a support system for your employees.** While an employee is learning a new skill, come up with structures that can support them. If they are challenged or have questions, who can they go to for help? Where can they find the answers? A clearly defined support system for people to know where they can go for help when they feel lost or frustrated is essential for developing new strengths. In David's case, we might set up a bi-weekly check-in to see how things are going and make sure he feels supported and encouraged.

3. **Try to reinforce growth by surrounding your employees with people who will support them in the development of their new skills**. As a leader, you need to serve as the model for the type of skills you are helping your employees learn. Alternatively, if you are not the best model for a particular skill, you shouldn't be afraid to point out the team member who is. If, for example, your employee is trying to become better at customer service, you'd want them to shadow your best customer service representative for a week—whether or not that's you.

A deficit-based mindset is not only likely to demotivate and undermine the growth of employees, but it also may inadvertently disrupt employees' trust in your leadership and future feedback. Altogether, deficit-based mindsets reduce performance, limit growth potential, and curb the psychological safety within your organization.

This is why cultivating a strength-based mindset is so important for Peaceful Leaders. Understanding how you think and talk about other people's communication styles, work products, behaviors, or communication has a lasting influence on your team—for better or for worse. Appreciation and a strength-based mindset that focuses on possibilities and growth can inspire hope and confidence in the future, while at the same time increasing Psychological Safety, Employee Trust, and Inclusion.

Best Practices for Employee Reviews

In every organization, no matter how big or small, employees need regular feedback—they need to know what they are doing well and where they need to improve. If they are not given feedback and therefore not given a chance to improve, that's a leadership problem, *not* an employee problem.

When it comes to more formal feedback, such as employee reviews, many organizations have set internal practices, policies, and procedures; they may be tied to promotional opportunities, merit raises, and/or your company's community principles and code of conduct. Some smaller organizations, on the other hand, do not hold regular or formal reviews. In any event, conducting reviews through a lens of appreciation is paramount to maintaining employee trust, safety, and inclusion.

An employee review can either be an extremely unpleasant experience or a truly valuable and welcomed opportunity. That's because being evaluated or appraised, especially if done ineffectively, can feel like a direct threat to our fundamental needs for respect, identity, safety, and control. Many of us in this situation will naturally engage in what author Sheila Heen refers to in *The Art of Receiving Feedback* as "Wrong Spotting"—meaning the receiver is coming into a feedback conversation ready to spot the ways you're wrong and defend or refute your feedback.

Your feedback is only as good as the receiver's ability to hear it. You can give feedback in the best way possible, but if they disagree with you or reject what you have to say, nothing will change, and it will strain your relationship and undermine their motivation and engagement in the future. This is why it's so important to implement best practices for turning employee reviews into valuable, pleasant experiences, where individuals leave feeling more optimistic and positive than they did before the review began.

The Peaceful Leadership five key principles for employee reviews help you turn reviews into a DANCE: **Dialogue, Appreciation, No Surprises, Coaching, and**

Evaluation. As we review them in the sections to follow, make sure to put them into practice in accordance with your own organization's procedures.

When facilitating employee reviews, incorporate the DANCE sequence

Dialogue	Make the review a 2-way dialogue, not a one-sided critique. A review should be an opportunity to reflect on the review period together.	
Appreciation	Employees should look forward to the review because it is an opportunity to feel seen and honored for the work they do.	
No Surprises	A review should be just that, a review of the feedback given and the professional accomplishments throughout the year.	
Coaching	Support their growth as an employee and professional by offering different strategies they might apply to their job.	
Evaluation	Help the employee understand how you came to your evaluation by offering specific examples that illustrate your evaluations.	

Dialogue

An employee review should be an opportunity to reflect on the challenges and successes of the review period, which should be a conversation, not a one-sided lecture. To promote this dialogue, try to create space for employees to share what they could use more or less of from you and the organization to help them thrive in their roles. Not only will this encourage a back-and-forth, but it will also promote durability and long-term success for the employee and the organization.

Your feedback is only effective insofar as your team member has buy-in— otherwise, they won't be motivated to take action. Instead of telling them what you think they can improve on, try sharing your feedback and asking for their thoughts. You can always sprinkle in your comments as the conversation progresses, but your employee will be more likely to hear and respond to your feedback if they are given a chance to participate and share their perspective with you. For example, rather than simply telling your employees you want them to take more ownership, you may phrase the feedback this way: "I thought there was some room for you to take more ownership of cross-functional projects. What are your thoughts on that?"

Be open to actually hearing and considering their response. Do not come in with an unspoken agenda that is rigid and unaffected by what you hear. Dialogue is ideally one-part talking and two-part listening. If you present your perspective and then listen carefully to their response, you will collaborate on changes that the employee buys into since they took part in creating the changes. You will also build on safety, trust, and inclusion, ultimately making your feedback much more effective now and in the future.

Appreciation

Appreciation should be the foundation of any employee review. Employees should look forward to the review as an opportunity to feel seen and honored for the work they do, which increases buy-in and improves receptivity to hard-to-hear feedback.

Remember to bring your strength-based mindset into the conversation. Focus on acknowledging their strengths, and when you need to bring up areas of improvement, focus on skills and information, not a lack of talent.

You can also bring appreciation into the review by celebrating successes. Be specific! Saying, "I appreciate what you do," doesn't show people their value. In fact, it can come across as superficial and even dismissive. If you want to share with someone that you value and appreciate them, start by sharing your observations of a specific behavior, event, or pattern that makes a positive impact on the organization's mission. For example: "I noticed that on the Johnson account, you really went out of your way to meet the needs of the client by getting them the extra numbers in the annual report. Great work!"

Appreciation satisfies our RISC needs and encourages people to continue growing and developing with the organization. Your employee review should consistently circle back to this principle.

No Surprises

No one likes to be caught off-guard or blindsided. A review should be just that: a *review* of professional accomplishments and feedback already given throughout the year.

Even so, one simple way to avoid catching people off-guard is by sending out an agenda in advance. Take the key questions or topics that you need to cover and send them out to the employee prior to their review. Encourage them to reflect on and prepare to discuss those items. (Of course, you should take time to prepare as well.)

Most importantly, practice giving feedback on a regular basis so that during a more formal review process, you can focus on reviewing the feedback already given. If you haven't already brought it up to your employee, it most likely should *not* be discussed in the employee review. Employees often come into a review meeting on edge about being evaluated; consequently, saving your more difficult feedback until this conversation is not a good practice. Instead, hold regular meetings throughout the year to give yourself an opportunity to bring up issues in a timely manner.

Coaching

Offer coaching where appropriate by suggesting alternative ways of doing things or talking through challenges to support the employee's growth. When coaching, refrain from telling the employee what to do and instead offer suggestions or ask insightful questions that help them think through similar situations in the future. This will help them evaluate different options and give them more control over their growth and performance. (Review Chapter 6 for more tips and tools to use during coaching conversations.)

Evaluation

It is human nature to want to know how we're doing, but how big of a role evaluations play in your employee review process depends on your company's practices and procedures. Whatever your internal procedures are regarding evaluations—whether they involve a rating system or some other criteria—it is essential to utilize and follow those specific guidelines for evaluations and to apply them consistently across employees and review periods. If you are not consistent in how you apply your evaluations between your employees or over the years, your employees will likely stop taking your evaluations seriously.

When you give an evaluation, it is incredibly important to help the employee understand how you came to your evaluation; that you give specific examples illustrating why you're giving the evaluation; and that you invite comments, questions, and concerns about any and all evaluations. If you give an employee a 4 out of 5, for example, you should be able to clearly explain your evaluation, provide examples, and explain what they can do in the next review period to get a 5 out of 5.

Employee reviews can be conversations people dread. That is NOT what we want. If you incorporate a strengths-based mindset and the DANCE principles into your review practices, you will slowly shift how your team experiences employee reviews. They will trust and respect you more, experience a greater sense of psychological safety within the team and organization, and feel included in the feedback process and their professional growth and development. The mark of a truly effective, Peaceful Leader is a team that actually looks forward to these reviews.

Case Narrative: Appreciation

When asked about feedback, Renee laughed. She shared that the only time she gets feedback on her work is when there's a problem. As she was reminded of the write-up (which was rescinded from HR), she said, "We get these pieces of paper that let us know there's an issue." Disciplinary action is valid in certain circumstances, but *corrective* action gives employees an opportunity to learn, transform, and grow. From Renee's perspective, she lacked the **appreciation** that would enable her to better receive constructive feedback. According to Connor, WDP Warehouse had annual performance reviews, which, he admitted, weren't very in-depth. There was clearly a need to normalize feedback and enhance appreciation at WDP Warehouse.

Looking deeper into their dynamic, we came to find that Renee and Connor's **deficit-based mindsets** continued to reinforce the narratives they told themselves about one another. Connor told himself that Renee was a complainer, always looking for a problem, and he subsequently tended to focus on the instances when Renee vented about issues while disregarding instances when Renee proactively found solutions to problems. This led to increased frustration on Connor's part and the tendency to dismiss the issues she brought up.

Then, Renee told herself that Connor played favorites and treated her more dismissively because she was a woman. She subsequently only paid attention to the times she felt dismissed and often forgot about the times when Connor attended thoughtfully to her concerns.

Throughout our process of coaching both Connor and Renee, we asked them both to start noticing the times that challenged their current views. We tasked Connor with recognizing and recording instances when Renee was proactive in solving problems, and we tasked Renee with recognizing and recording when Connor was attentive to her. We also asked each of them to spend a few days thinking about, noticing, and writing down any other strengths they noticed in the other.

Both began to increase their **strength-based mindset** and appreciation towards one another, which altered the way they thought, felt, and behaved. Soon, Connor was able to **reframe** Renee's complaints as opportunities to learn about operational challenges in the warehouse, to become aware of his own blind spots, and to collaboratively problem-solve. And Renee was able to reframe Connor's attention to others as a greater trust in her work ethic and competence, leaving her with more autonomy. She began noticing when he was attentive toward her, and she was feeling increasingly more appreciative of his attention. They both had more to work on, of course, but viewing each other through a strengths-based mindset began to significantly improve their appreciation for one another.

STRATEGY SESSION

Okay, let's see how you can be more appreciative of your team. See if you can finish the following sentences.

I would be a more appreciative leader if I......

If I did that, I would be more effective as a leader because......

A challenge for me to grow in this area is.....

To overcome this challenge, I can......

My first step to being a more appreciative leader is......

CHAPTER 8

Curiosity

Within the organizational literature, **curiosity** relates to a general capacity for and enjoyment of learning[36] as well as an open-mindedness to new information (as opposed to defensiveness).[37] Behaviors related to curiosity include observing, asking questions, and seeking knowledge, all of which help reduce group conflict and increase more effective group processes.[38,39]

---

[36] Lievens, F., Harrison, S. H., Mussel, P., & Litman, J. A. (2022). Killing the cat? A review of curiosity at work. *Academy of Management Annals, 16(1)*, 179-216.

[37] Taylor, S. N., & Bright, D. S. (2011). Open-mindedness and defensiveness in multisource feedback processes: A conceptual framework. *The Journal of Applied Behavioral Science, 47(4)*, 432-460.

[38] Gino, F. (2018). Why curiosity matters?. *Harvard Business Review, September-October issue*, 47-61.

[39] Horstmeyer, A. (2020). The generative role of curiosity in soft skills development for contemporary VUCA environments. *Journal of Organizational Change Management, 33(5)*, 737-751.

As Peacebuilders who support workplaces around the world dealing with difficult and escalated dynamics, the skills discussed in this chapter have been essential for our conflict resolution processes. In our experience, curiosity can transform challenging situations and conflicts into opportunities for growth.

In this chapter, you'll learn how to deal with and de-escalate heightened workplace situations, address and give feedback on difficult behaviors, and mediate employee issues—all through the lens of curiosity. If implemented effectively, these skills will bolster the three pillars of psychological safety, employee trust, and inclusion in your organization.

De-escalation Skills Using the C.A.R.E.S. Sequence

Escalation is the label we use to describe a combination of psychological, physiological, and behavioral phenomena, including threat perception, heightened nervous system arousal, and defensive behaviors. When we are emotionally escalated, a variety of interesting things are happening in our bodies and minds. Our sympathetic nervous system is hyperactivated, causing a flood of hormones that increase heart rate, breathing, and blood pressure, which trigger a variety of emotions, such as nervousness, anxiety, anger, fear, and/or hopelessness, among others. Unable to access our higher-functioning cognitive abilities, we instead resort to a fight/flight/freeze response, which results in behaviors like arguing, attacking, avoiding, or totally shutting down.

We've all experienced emotional escalation from time to time, and we've all been with others who have escalated because of something we said or did. In this state, it is virtually impossible to reason with someone or get them to participate in any sort of creative problem-solving. This is why it's so important to recognize when someone (e.g., a team member or customer) is emotionally escalated or *triggered* and how to use certain de-escalation tactics. These techniques help reduce an individual's perception of threat and increase their feeling of safety, thereby allowing their nervous system to return to a calmer state—at which point reasoning and problem-solving become possible again.

So, what exactly is under "threat" when people become escalated at work? Typically, this question leads back to our basic psychological needs. When someone's RISC needs are threatened or impeded, or even perceived to be so, emotional escalation is a natural consequence. And if you, as a leader, are ever accused as the cause and/or target of a team member's escalation, it may be easy for you to escalate as well.

To reduce the threat to someone's RISC needs and turn a potentially negative situation into an opportunity for growth, we can follow our CARES de-escalation sequence. CARES stands for....

- Calmly listen

- Align and acknowledge
- Reassure
- Explain your needs
- Suggest possible solutions

Consider the following scenario. Maria and Patrick are each director-level employees in different departments, but they collaborate quite regularly in cross-functional initiatives and projects. In one department meeting, Maria suggested an idea on how to cut down costs and increase efficiency within Patrick's department. After the meeting, Patrick approached Maria with a lot of intensity, which caught Maria off-guard.

Patrick exclaimed, "Maria, don't you ever call me out in a meeting like that again. Why don't you just mind your own business!"

Now, if Maria were not a Peaceful Leader, she might have reacted and said, "Well, if you could take care of your department, I wouldn't have to tell you what to do!" Most likely, this would've led to a breakdown of psychological safety, trust, and inclusion, increasing the escalation and fracturing the relationship between the two.

Thankfully, however, Maria is a Peaceful Leader. She remembered to use the STOP strategy discussed in Chapter 5 to collect herself. She then proceeded with her CARES de-escalation sequence to reduce the tension in the situation.

After Patrick approached Maria, she first took a deep breath. She then wanted to make sure she fully understood where Patrick was coming from before responding. She started with the first CARES tool and **calmly listened** until Patrick was done confronting her. Then, she said, "Patrick, I can hear what I said in the meeting upset you. This is the last thing I wanted. Can you tell me a bit more about how my suggestions affected you or what they seemed to imply?"

Notice that Maria didn't dismiss Patrick's perception but rather took it seriously, deciding to truly *care* about his experience. She began by becoming curious and gathering information to better understand where Patrick was coming from. Even though her communication was not intentionally hurtful, she realized that Patrick interpreted it as such. By calmly listening and seeking to understand, Maria was able to get more information and let Patrick vent a bit, which helped him feel like he was being cared for (i.e., safe), laying the foundation for a constructive dialogue.

Ultimately, Maria learned that Patrick had been under pressure from their Vice President to make improvements in his department. He had been doing everything he could but didn't have the support or resources he felt he needed. During their exchange, he perceived Maria as withholding resources from him because he thought she wanted him to fail. Underlying Patrick's escalation was a threat to his RISC needs. He was clearly feeling a lack of *respect* from his boss and a lack of *control* to address the issues without the appropriate resources.

This was all new to Maria, and hearing this helped her understand how best to proceed. She then took the next step in the CARES sequence: **Acknowledge and Align.** Accordingly, she acknowledged Patrick's concerns and expressed their aligned interests. She responded, "So, you're feeling a lot of pressure right now to make improvements in your department, and my comments clearly added to that feeling for you. That was certainly not my intention. In fact, I want you to feel supported and have the resources you need."

Notice how Maria first acknowledged Patrick's concerns by repeating or paraphrasing what she heard from him. Then, she aligned with his interests by showing she shared the same goals and concerns. When you're aligning with someone, do so in a way that is appropriate and authentic. If you fake alignment just to get the person to calm down, there's a good chance it will come off as condescending, which might escalate the situation further.

Subsequently, Maria brought in the **reassure step** of the CARES sequence to make Patrick feel confident that there would be a positive path forward and that she could be seen as an ally, not an enemy. She continued, "I would really like to see if I can offer some support and work through this together. Can we sit down this afternoon and brainstorm some options?"

Patrick became noticeably calmer and agreed to talk with Maria further. By scheduling a specific time to discuss

Patrick's concerns, she communicated to him that she was taking his needs seriously and, at the same time, creating space between the escalation and the problem-solving conversation. This space would help reduce tensions further by allowing each of them time to approach the conversation professionally and respectfully.

Later that afternoon, Maria and Patrick sat down to discuss options. At that point, however, Maria was feeling a bit hurt from the encounter herself; she didn't really feel like she was able to express her needs earlier because she was so focused on de-escalating Patrick. But Maria knew her needs matter, too. So, Maria turned to the last two tools of the CARES sequence, **explaining her needs** and **suggesting possible solutions**.

Seeing as the situation had de-escalated to a place where Maria felt she could share her needs without risking re-escalation, she decided to start the meeting with what was on her mind so she could move forward with a clear head: "Patrick, I really appreciate you bringing up your concerns to me this morning. The last thing I would ever want is for you to think I'm trying to make you look bad or undermine your success. I respect you too much for that. At the same time, when you approached me after the meeting, I felt a bit disrespected myself. I want you to be able to come to me with issues like this in the future, but I need it to happen in a different way. Can we agree to approach each other privately next time and give each other the benefit of the doubt before jumping to assumptions?" Patrick agreed, so Maria continued: "Thanks, Patrick. Now, I have some ideas on how to share some resources with you. Would love to get your thoughts on this…"

By implementing the CARES de-escalation sequence and approaching the escalated interaction with curiosity, Maria was not only able to de-escalate the situation but also develop trust with Patrick, promote safety for him to be able to raise concerns with her in the future and allow him to feel included in finding a more constructive way to communicate. De-escalating is all about putting *care* first and *solution* second.

Addressing Difficult Behavior

As a leader, you likely have to address difficult, frustrating, or inappropriate behavior from employees on occasion. Delivering hard-to-hear feedback to people can be quite uncomfortable for everyone involved and potentially lead to escalation. In these situations, however, curiosity has the capacity to transform difficult conversations into opportunities for growth.

Remember, our goal in giving feedback is to promote changes in behavior and communication that better serve the team and the organization as a whole. That said, people rarely view their own behavior as challenging or difficult—it's human nature to see our own actions and communications in a positive light. As Peaceful Leaders, then, it's crucial that we focus on delivering feedback in a way that minimizes defensiveness and encourages curiosity from all parties. Change only happens if the person receiving feedback understands and agrees to that the changes being asked of them are valuable. For leaders, curiosity helps us identify the underlying strengths of an employee's seemingly undesirable behavior; for employees, curiosity facilitates open-mindedness and understanding.

In the following sections, we'll outline some general best practices for giving feedback. Then, we'll go over a specific process you can use to deliver feedback effectively.

Best Practices for Delivering Feedback

Firstly, Peaceful Leaders should offer feedback *regularly*. Feedback doesn't have to be critical or constructive; in fact, we should be delivering positive feedback (i.e., feedback that reinforces valued behavior) at least five or six times more often than negative feedback (i.e., feedback that prompts changes to problematic behavior). This makes it easier to offer difficult feedback in the future. In general, we call this filling up our **trust bank**. If our trust bank account is full, we can make withdrawals (i.e., deliver critical feedback) without breaking our employee's trust.

Secondly, we need to offer feedback in a *timely manner*. Waiting to give someone feedback makes it harder to address the issues with them constructively. This is partly because we forget 50 to 80% of new information three days after an event occurs.[40] What feels like accurate recollections of events are often skewed by biased reconstructions, which typically favor our self-perception. So, the longer we wait to give feedback, the more distorted both our view and the employee's view of the behavior will be—and the harder it will be to discuss the situation productively. Delayed feedback might also catch people off-guard, which can lead to feelings of resentment (e.g., "You've been holding onto that all this time and didn't say anything?").

Finally, when we give feedback, we should offer *specific observations* rather than general descriptions, labels, or evaluations. Our feedback should also include *actionable suggestions* to help the employee grow. Implementing these practices will not only help feedback conversations go more smoothly but, over time, will also improve your relationships.

Sequence for Delivering Feedback

To deliver feedback even more effectively, you can implement a particular conversation sequence that embodies these best practices, keeps the conversation from becoming escalated, and ushers everyone towards a solution. We call this the BiEAR sequence:

- Behavior
- interpretation

---

[40] Murre, J. M., & Dros, J. (2015). Replication and analysis of Ebbinghaus' forgetting curve. *PloS one*, *10*(7), e0120644.

- Effect
- Ask
- Request or Resolution

Before we dive into the specifics of the BiEAR process, we need to remember to frame the conversation in a way that minimizes defensiveness. **Framing** is one of the most important parts of giving hard-to-hear feedback. Always start with something positive if you can, and paint a picture of why your feedback could be beneficial. Do your best to bring in a strength-based mindset in your framing. You'll also want to bring in some of your CARES de-escalation skills from earlier in the chapter.

Here is a framing example: "Sam, I'm really pleased to see the progress you and the team are making on the California project. Do you have a few minutes to check in? I just wanted to talk to you about how yesterday's meeting went because I really care about your success on the initiative. Do you mind if I share my perspective with you?"

Notice in this opening that we are checking for time constraints so we can discover whether this is an appropriate time to bring up our feedback. By clearly stating the topic, we're making sure we don't catch Sam off-guard. We're also aligning with her interests (i.e., success on the project), which can mitigate defensiveness. And finally, we're getting her permission before we start sharing our perspective.

Once we have this permission, we want to share our feedback through the BiEAR framework, starting with the observed **behavior**, our **interpretation**, and the **effect** it has on us or others. It's important to separate the *observed* behavior from our *interpretation* of that behavior, as the two may or may not be the same.

For example, we might say to Sam, "In the meeting yesterday, when you asked Eliana a question in the middle of her presentation, it seemed to me that she was thrown off by your comments and perhaps a bit irritated by the interruption. I know you are going to need her support on this project for it to be successful, and I'm concerned about the effect that interruption may have had on her."

Instead of saying that Sam interrupted Eliana, we present the behavior without judgment by simply describing it as it was observed: Sam asking a question. Only then do we let her know our interpretation of the interruption and the effect it may have had. This way, Sam can save face—we're not judging her, attacking her, or questioning her character; we're simply drawing her attention to the impact of her behavior. After we state the behavior, interpretation, and effect, we want to **Ask** or open a dialogue to understand her perspective better. This gives Sam an opportunity to clarify her side of the situation, which helps meet Sam's RISC needs. For example, we might ask, "What was going on for you during Eliana's presentation?" or "How did you perceive Eliana reacting to your question?"

Creating space for the other person to respond is a much more inclusive way of delivering feedback. Within this space, we should expect (and hope for) a dialogue where we can continue to use curiosity to better understand the situation and the employee's behavior.

Once we have the requisite information and a firm grasp of the situation, we can make a **request** or propose a **resolution**. Continuing with the same scenario, let's say we learn that Sam is simply excited about the project and that her enthusiasm manifested itself in an unintended fashion. Knowing this, we might say: "It's great to hear how passionate you are about this project. Of course, we also need you and Eliana to be on good terms moving forward for the project to be successful. Would you be willing to swing by her office today just to check in with her?"

Alternatively, let's say we found out that Sam interrupted Eliana not because of her excitement but because she felt Eliana was stealing her ideas. In this situation, we might make the following request or proposal: "I wouldn't feel good either if I felt someone was trying to steal my ideas. Sam, we need you and Eliana to be on the same page for this project. So, if you need to address something with her, it would be great for you to do so directly and privately or come to me for support instead of airing things out in front of the team. Can we try that moving forward?" If she agrees, we might say: "Okay, thank you. What support do you need to clear things up with Eliana to get back on track? How can I help?"

Often, when it comes to difficult situations in the workplace, we forget that our employees are human beings with feelings, goals, and underlying concerns that drive their behavior. As a Peaceful Leader, inserting curiosity into the conversation allows you to bring the motivations and concerns of all parties to the surface; as a result, you and your employee can find a mutually agreeable path forward.

Mediating Coworker Conflict

Take a minute and think about a time when two or more of your team members were in conflict, and it was up to you to facilitate some sort of conversation or solution. Did it stress you out? Did you wish they could just work it out on their own? Were you feeling frustrated that you had to spend time managing this?

Employee conflict can be one of the most stressful situations for a leader. However, if asked to identify some positive outcomes from conflicts you've helped solve, you would probably be able to come up with a few examples. Taking a *curious* approach to employee conflict can help us create and find opportunities that increase Employee Trust, Psychological Safety, and Inclusion. Below, you'll find a five-step process for mediating employee conflict that can help you and your team create opportunities for growth when conflicts emerge.

Mediating Employee Conflict Checklist

Step 1: Discovery

- [ ] Meet with each party to gather information.
- [ ] De-escalate as needed.
  - ○ Calmly Listen.
  - ○ Acknowledge their experience and confirm understanding.
  - ○ Instill confidence in the future.
- [ ] AVOID making commitments or decisions until you gathered information from all appropriate sources and perspectives.
- [ ] Elicit buy-in on how to proceed.
  - ○ Is mediation voluntary or mandatory?
  - ○ Who needs to be involved?

Step 2: Story Telling

- [ ] Ensure everyone is available and fully present for the duration of the meeting.
- [ ] Give each party some uninterrupted time to share their story.
- [ ] Encourage listening parties to focus on trying to understand, not for rebuttal.
  - ○ Have them repeat back what they heard to be important to the sharing party.
- [ ] Intervene when necesssary to:
  - ○ Ensure each party has uniterrupted time to share.
  - ○ To ask clarifying questions.
  - ○ To summarize the key points of what was shared to ensure a common. understanding for the parties involved.

Step 3: Make an Agenda

☐ Make an agenda by eliciting the main items that are important to talk about.
☐ Hold your suggestions until the end to promote the parties ownership of the conversation.
☐ Use the agenda as a roadmap to keep everyone focused and on track.

Step 4: Discuss

☐ Invite the parties to use the agenda and to work together to find resolutions and new understandings.
☐ Let them lead the conversation from here (sometimes at this point, they might be able to figure it out on their own). They will be more likely to follow through with agreements if they take ownership over the dialogue.
☐ If things start to get stuck or escalated, try the following intervention tools:
  ○ CARES and BiEAR - Remember these sequences from earlier in the Curiosity Module can help you de-escalate the situation or offer feedback.
  ○ Focus on interests - Ask questions to help parties get to the underlying interests (or their why) of their positions and issues. Once you have identified the underlying interests encourage problem-solving at an interest level.
  ○ Focus on future action - In mediation you have to balance reconciling the past with moving toward the future. Make sure everyone has a chance to feel heard about the past, but avoid getting stuck on what has happened and help them start to think about what this means for the future.
  ○ Take a break - Sometimes you just need a break if things are not working. You might meet with people individually during the break to offer coaching or feedback.

Step 5: Promote Accountability

☐ When agreements or new understandings are made, elicit tangible action items and who will be doing what, when, where, and how to ensure clarity and accountability.
☐ If appropriate, draft up agreements or a summary (formally or informally) for everyone to refer back to.
☐ If appropriate, schedule a follow-up conversation about 3-6 weeks from now to check in and adjust agreements.

Step 1: Discovery

Before you decide how to handle an employee dispute, you need to gather the necessary information. In the discovery phase, meet with each person involved individually, bringing a curious mindset to understand their perspectives. Seek clarity on each individual's needs, concerns, and ideas for resolution. If those involved in the conflict are emotionally triggered or extremely defensive, you may first have to de-escalate heightened emotions by deploying the CARES sequence discussed earlier in this chapter.

Although you may begin to discuss possible solutions with each individual, be careful not to make firm plans for moving forward until you've heard from all the parties involved. If you commit to a solution without hearing the whole story, you may find the commitments or solutions are unrealistic or don't actually resolve the issue; in turn, you'd likely be intervening from a biased perspective, aligning yourself with one employee over another, which could undermine your credibility as a trustworthy mediator. At this stage, simply focus on acknowledging each person's experience, gathering information, and instilling confidence with regard to a constructive path forward.

If, while meeting with the necessary parties, you hear something that would trigger a formal procedure, like harassment, discrimination, or other rule violations relevant to your workplace or industry, make sure to follow the appropriate steps internally before resolving the issue alone and informally. However, if this is an informal, non-legal conflict, and you are the appropriate person to support a conversation, ask the parties if they would agree to a meeting in which you would serve as the mediator or facilitator. It's important for you to be clear about whether you're inviting your team members to voluntarily attend this meeting or requiring they attend as part of their job. If it's optional, and one or more parties do not want to participate, you might want to coach the team members individually to reach a resolution. In the steps to follow, however, we will assume all parties have agreed to participate in a dialogue.

As you bring people together, make sure everyone is clear on how much time they should reserve on their calendars. Also, make sure that the dialogue is held in a private location – preferably somewhere neutral (i.e., a conference room) and not one of the individual's offices.

Step 2: Storytelling

Storytelling is a crucial first step in the workplace mediation process as it allows all parties to gain a deeper understanding of the situation from each other's perspective. By sharing their stories, individuals can uncover the assumptions and biases that may have been driving their behavior and decision-making. This process can lead to greater empathy and understanding between parties and help to identify common ground for resolving the conflict. By acknowledging and challenging the stories they tell themselves, individuals can create new, more positive narratives and move forward toward a more productive and harmonious working environment.

With that being said, start by giving each party a chance to share their perspective without interruption. Encourage the party not to share but to focus on listening and understanding where the other person is coming from. You may even have the listener repeat what they heard and ask clarifying questions that could help them understand the other person's perspective.

Only intervene if the listener interrupts or if you want to ask a clarifying question to the person sharing. You may also want to briefly summarize the key points that each person said to help ensure that everyone present understands the key points or issues.

Step 3: Make an Agenda

After everyone has had a chance to share their stories, ask them to make a list of the items that *need* to be discussed in order to move beyond the conflict. If you have items that *you* want reflected on the agenda, try to withhold them until the parties have finished putting their joint list together. This promotes a sense of ownership over the topics they want to discuss.

Once they have their agendas, you'll want to review them for appropriateness and clarity. If anything is unclear, try to get your employees to be more specific about behaviors or processes that aren't working for them. It's also a good practice to separate the behaviors identified from the *interpretations* placed on those behaviors. If, for example, one of the parties writes "Mike's rude behavior at meetings" as an agenda item, you'll want to help them identify which specific behaviors are problematic (e.g., interrupting others, yelling, etc.) and separate them from the interpretations of that behavior (e.g., Mike is rude, doesn't respect my opinion, he wants to intimidate me, etc.).

Once the agenda is clear, with specific behaviors or processes identified as challenges, use the agenda to make sure everyone stays on track during the discussion.

Step 4: Discuss

Using the agenda, invite the participants to work together to find resolutions and new understandings on their agenda. You will be involved in the discussion as well, but try to let them take the lead. You might be surprised at their ability to work things out on their own with simply your presence for support. They will also be more likely to follow through with agreements if they take ownership of the conversation. As the conversation progresses, here are some key mediation skills you can use to aid the discussion.

Mediation Skill #1: CARES De-escalation Tools and BiEAR Feedback Tools

Make sure that you use your CARES de-escalation sequence discussed earlier in the chapter to help keep the tensions manageable and the conversation professional. And when you need to offer feedback, remember to use the BiEAR feedback tools, also previously discussed in this chapter. When delivering feedback, remember to consider timing and location (e.g., it may be more appropriate to deliver some feedback privately).

Mediation Skill #2: Focus on Interests

When positions, requests, or proposals are made that not everyone can agree to, encourage people to dive deeper and explore the interests or needs underneath their communications, behaviors, or proposed solutions. For example, if Craig wants to communicate primarily via email and Mason wants to communicate primarily in person, you might ask: "What about those proposals that are important to you? Why is it important for you to communicate via email?"

Once you get down to the underlying interests—the *why* beneath the *what* —you may be able to help redirect the conversation from their original conflicting positions to a more aligned proposal that satisfies each person's underlying needs. Focusing on underlying interests or needs rather than on surface-level positions or desires affords us the ability to get creative in problem-solving. In fact, we might be able to satisfy each person's core needs in a way that has nothing to do with their starting positions.

For example, let's say Craig wants to communicate via email because it allows him to process information before responding, and Mason wants to communicate face-to-face because he finds it to be more efficient. You could pose the question: "How can you two communicate in a way that is both efficient and allows time for individual processing?"

This new frame for the conversation may help them approach the dialogue from a creative and collaborative problem-solving mindset rather than trying to convince the other why their own idea is right and the other's is wrong. You may also find that focusing on underlying interests allows for parties to discover common ground, and you can build from there rather than from a place of difference.

Mediation Skill #3: Focus on Future Action

As the discussion continues, encourage everyone to think about what they want moving forward. Don't dismiss people's feelings about what *has* happened—help them feel heard about the past and *then* move the conversation towards a future-focused goal or vision that prioritizes mutual understanding and actionable agreements.

Mediation Skill #4: Take a Break

If the conversation escalates at any point, you may want to take a break to let things simmer down. Don't force a discussion if the conversation is turning unprofessional, disrespectful, or unproductive. Instead, give everyone some time to breathe.

You could take a short 15- or 30-minute break to simply reset for continued discussion. Or you might want to take a longer break and convene on a different day. Just make sure everyone knows when you are reconvening so they can plan accordingly and feel accountable for continuing the dialogue. You could also schedule 1-on-1 meetings with your team members before reconvening to check in and offer private coaching to help them be more effective in the next conversation.

Step 5: Promote Accountability

In this final phase, encourage turning the discussion into action items and tangible changes. How will their communication or collaborations change? How will their behaviors change? How will they know when things have changed? What will their agreements or new understandings look like in action? Help them explore how to handle potential future challenges should similar situations arise.

If appropriate, draft up agreements and understandings in a document or email to which everyone can refer back. Schedule a follow-up meeting two to four weeks after the conversation to check in on how things are going. If necessary, continue having follow-up conversations with the parties to promote sustainable and long-term success.

Addressing employee conflict is far from a science. Every situation is different and may need to be handled differently. However, treating employee conflict with curiosity, drawing on all of your other skills as a Peaceful Leader, and using this five-step process as a guide can help you be as effective as possible at finding opportunities within conflict. As a Peaceful Leader, mediating coworker conflicts should help increase the three pillars of psychological safety, employee trust, and inclusion in your workplace.

There were a lot of skills covered in this chapter, including the CARES de-escalation sequence, the BiEAR model for giving difficult feedback, and a 5-step process to mediate employee issues. Remember that as a Peaceful Leader, where others see conflict and potential challenges, we see opportunities to resolve underlying issues, repair and deepen relationships, and create a safe, trusting, and inclusive environment.

This is one chapter that you will definitely want to revisit for reminders and continued practice because these are some of the more challenging but most important skills a Peaceful Leader can learn and develop.

Case Narrative: Curiosity

At this point, Connor and Renee were both feeling a bit less tense and more appreciative of one another. But of course, there would still be instances where one of them aggravated the other, and many of the tools we've been working on were basically forgotten. For instance, even though Connor had now scheduled regular meetings, he did still occasionally call spontaneous meetings throughout the week. At this point, full trust between Renee and Connor had not yet been restored, so any instance of Renee being left out was triggering her need for belonging and identity as a valued member of the team. When Renee missed two meetings that Connor called, we encouraged her not to keep this to herself and stew on it. Rather, we helped her formulate her feedback using the BiEAR sequence.

A **BiEAR** message from Renee:	
Behavior	*"Conor, I've noticed you are still holding crew meetings when I'm not around. Like just last Wednesday, when you had that gathering to talk about new equipment, and I wasn't here, and this Monday when you got everyone together to check-in about the new training requirements…"*

interpretation	*"...The story I'm telling myself about this is that my role or contributions aren't important enough to be included..."*
Effect	*"... which causes me to question my role here and whether meetings are being held deliberately when I'm not around. I know this may not be the case, but it's the story that's going on in my head. It also left me unaware of the new training we need to take, which Raul had to inform me about."*
Ask	*"Did you realize I didn't have that information? Or that holding those meetings without me might make me feel this way?"*
Request	(After listening to Connor's response, she repeated back what she heard and made a request) ... *"Okay, so you were just super busy and didn't consider who was in or out of the meeting. I understand. It's not always easy to pay attention to all the information that everyone needs or has. Would it be possible, going forward, to set up some way of proactively getting me any information I*

> *might miss during impromptu meetings? Or maybe making a point to recap any information in our regularly scheduled all-team meetings?"*

This feedback led Renee and Connor to brainstorm a few ways to make the dissemination of new information easy and reasonable for Connor, keeping in mind how busy he usually was. Renee was also willing to be proactive and ask him what she may have missed while absent. The conversation also led Connor to realize that the dissemination and communication of new information across the team so that everyone was on the same page regularly was an issue at the company. He planned on bringing together some senior leaders to address the issue.

Due to Renee giving feedback and Connor being willing to listen with curiosity, she was able to feel heard and get her needs addressed, while Connor was able to recognize and attend to gaps in his and the company's communications. In other words, this small conflict turned into an opportunity for growth rather than a catalyst for mistrust and stress.

STRATEGY SESSION

Okay, let's see how you can be more curious with your team. See if you can finish the following sentences.

I would be a more curious leader if I......

If I did that, I would be more effective as a leader because......

A challenge for me to grow in this area is.....

To overcome this challenge, I can......

My first step to being a more curious leader is......

CHAPTER 9

Empowerment

As defined in the organizational literature, the competency of **empowerment** refers to a leader's ability to give their employees ownership over their work, a feeling that their opinions are heard and considered, and the confidence that they have what they need to be successful in their roles. As shown in a review of employee empowerment, empowered employees show greater work satisfaction, lower job strain, and better performance[41]; it also reduces perceptions of workplace incivility,[42]leading to more peaceful interactions and relationships. Ultimately, empowerment is essential in helping individuals feel that they have a stake in the

---

[41] Spreitzer, G. M., & Doneson, D. (2005). Musings on the past and future of employee empowerment. *Handbook of organizational development, 4*, 5-10.

[42] Smith, L. M., Andrusyszyn, M. A., & Spence Laschinger, H. K. (2010). Effects of workplace incivility and empowerment on newly-graduated nurses' organizational commitment. *Journal of Nursing Management, 18(8)*, 1004-1015.

organization's success, which makes them feel more accountable for the quality of their work.

In this chapter, you'll learn specific skills that we, as Peacebuilders, have found to be essential to empower employees across the workforce, including a robust process for inclusive decision-making and steps for promoting a culture of accountability. If implemented correctly, these tactics can enhance the three pillars of psychological safety, employee trust, and inclusion.

Inclusive Decision-Making

At the heart of empowerment is the ability to give team members a sense of agency while also weighing the competing needs and interests of the organization and its stakeholders. This balance can help leaders more often make fair, inclusive, and transparent decisions. Even in really difficult situations, where some people may feel devalued and angry, we must try to make decisions that will foster a sense of ownership over the direction of the organization and promote the three pillars of Peaceful Leadership. When people do not feel included in decisions that will ultimately affect them or disrupt their work, they will likely feel frustrated and disempowered, which leads to conflict.

Inclusive processes are a way to truly cultivate fairness in the organization, which is critical for maintaining trust and safety. So, how might a Peaceful Leader engage in an inclusive decision-making process, especially when one needs to make an unpopular decision? For starters, let's take a look at three principles of inclusive decision-making.

Key Principle #1: People Want to Be Heard

When we have to make decisions that are going to affect others, the individuals affected will want to share their perspectives and be involved in the decision-making process. Giving people a voice in the process is key to inclusive decision-making and serves their basic psychological need for control or agency. They may not all be satisfied with the ultimate outcome, but at the very least, they'll feel included and, hopefully, get a sense that you are weighing several perspectives and considerations before making decisions. The important distinction, in these cases, is that employees not only feel heard but also *considered*—that you're actually taking into account their input. So, before asking for input, make sure to give them as much information about the situation as you can.

Involving others in the decision-making process benefits not only your employees but also you and the organization. You never know who may come up with an idea or creative solution you hadn't thought of.

Key Principle #2: People Want Transparency

Sometimes, it's not possible to hear or consider everyone's ideas on a decision. Tough decisions might have to be made quickly or with limited input from others. And even if you do hear and consider everyone's ideas, there are bound to be some people who are not satisfied with the outcome. So, whatever the decision is, regardless of how it turns out, you'll want to be as clear and transparent about the factors that led to the decision, how the decision was made, and why you believe it is the right decision at this time. If people feel like they clearly understand how and why the decision was made, they'll be more likely to buy into it, even if they disagree initially.

Key Principle #3: People Want Accountability

Giving people an opportunity to voice their perspectives and having a transparent process is not sufficient if people don't trust that you're actually going to do what you say you're going to do and hold yourself accountable. Set clear expectations upfront regarding how you plan to implement the decision, how you'll know whether the decision is working, and when you're going to check back in with everyone to let them know the results and make adjustments as needed. No matter what, make it clear how you'll be responsible for implementing the decision and measuring its outcomes over the short- and long-term.

A tip: under certain circumstances, you might have made a decision quickly without soliciting much input; in this case, you might let people know that you'll try this direction for 90 days, after which point, if it isn't working, you'll have an all-hands meeting to consider the team's perspectives.

In the section to follow, we'll outline a specific five-step process for making inclusive decisions. If you put this into practice in your organization, do your best to keep these key principles in mind.

Step 1: Prepare for the Process

When you're about to make a decision that will affect others, especially in a significant and/or disruptive way, you'll want to do some preparation before bringing it to the team. Sit down with whomever else will be involved with making the final decision and decide how much information you can disclose to the entire team—regarding the factors leading to the situation, the possible options, and the potential challenges. Maybe you can be completely transparent and disclose all of it; maybe you can only share a portion.

You'll also want to decide how you'll go about gathering and considering input and how to articulate the process clearly to the team so they know what they can expect. You may even suggest a timeline for gathering input and a date for making a final decision.

It is also crucial to decide who, exactly, you are going to gather input from. Maybe it's the whole team, or maybe it's just a few key employees. In any event, remember to try to include the people who are actually going to be affected by the decision as often as possible.

Step 2: Gather Input, Including Underlying Interests

Now, it's time to carry out your plan. If the number of people involved in the decision-making process is reasonable, you might simply call a meeting. To open the meeting, tell them what's on the agenda, and, per what you prepared in Step 1, be as clear and transparent as possible about the entire situation.

After the disclosure, let them know you want their input before making any final decisions, and give each person some time—it could be just a minute or two each—to give feedback, present ideas, and ask questions. As you listen, don't evaluate any of the ideas. Simply repeat out loud and write down what you heard so each person knows you were listening and that all parties agree on what was said.

Let everyone speak and give input before moving into any sort of evaluative discussion. This step can be a brainstorming exercise—total freedom to voice perspectives, beliefs, goals, concerns, and ideas without any sort of judgment. If it's reasonable, given the allotted time for the meeting, you might then move into the next step, evaluation, which we'll discuss below. If not, you'll want to give everyone your next steps timeline: how long it will take you to consider the options and ideas you heard, what the next step will be, and when it will take place.

If the number of people involved is too large for a live discussion, you might send out an anonymous survey. You could, again, clearly present the issue and factors that led to the situation, this time in writing at the opening of the survey. Then, you can present the options you've been considering (e.g., as multiple-choice options) and let people choose which they most prefer. You'll also want to include some open-ended questions so that you can get their feedback, ideas, and questions. In the survey or the email that sends the survey link, let everyone know your decision process timeline: when you would like responses, when and what the next step is, and when you would like to make a final decision. An anonymous survey could also be a good idea even after you've had a live discussion, as it's typically a good idea to offer a confidential avenue for people to share their thoughts in the event they don't feel safe to do so publicly.

Whether running a survey or a meeting, give everyone some direction as to whom they can talk to during the decision-making process (i.e., in between meetings). Especially with disruptive decisions, people may feel anxious, frustrated, or confused. You'll want to give them an outlet for expressing this and asking further questions; otherwise, they are bound to create narratives and assumptions about the future, which could deteriorate their sense of trust and safety with you and your organization.

Finally, when gathering input on potential decisions that will affect several stakeholders, a Peaceful Leader will focus on *interests*, not solutions. Although the goal is to get to solutions and decisions, we want to start with interests in order to foster a creative and inclusive atmosphere within the process. In this context, interests are the underlying needs, goals, values, motives, expectations, and/or perceptions that drive our positions or proposed solutions. Some people in your organization might, for example, come to work because they really need the benefits; others come because they really connect with the company's mission and values. The fact of the matter is, unless you have a strong pulse on your people's underlying interests, values, and perspectives, you're probably just guessing when it comes to what will truly satisfy or destabilize them. When you give people a voice, ask about the *why* underneath their input to get a clear sense of the interests, goals, values, and motives that might be driving their opinions.

Step 3: Evaluate Ideas

Once you have an understanding of which decisions people would like to see made and why, you can begin to collectively evaluate what you heard. Again, you can do this through a meeting or town hall or else through a survey that exposes certain themes, interests, and options from the initial survey.

One way of going about idea evaluation is to engage in a *divergent-convergent* thinking approach. The divergent-convergent decision-making model encourages you to separate brainstorming (the previous step) from the idea-refinement stage (the current step).

To start, use the ideas and underlying interests you heard in the previous step and combine the most prominent ones by using the following framework: "How can we _____ (insert an interest), while at the same time _____ (insert a different interest)?"

Let's say we're trying to make a decision as to where we can cut personnel-related expenses. And through our meetings, surveys, and focus groups, two of the main underlying interests we heard were a need for healthcare and a fear of reentering the job market. For the purposes of this book, we are obviously simplifying a complex dynamic. But let's take these interests and start a divergent process by using the aforementioned framework. We can come up with a question like this: "How can we continue to provide healthcare while at the same time keeping everyone's job safe using the available budget?"

Now, we have a problem statement that promotes creativity and a focus on underlying interests, which we can use to generate a list of options. Perhaps we can come up with ideas like:

- Voluntary layoffs with severance
- Temporary reduction in non-medical care benefits
- A furlough program spread out over a year to minimize the impact on the employee

We can continue to combine interests to create new problem statements and generate additional options. We should do this until we feel like we have a robust list of options that we can start developing and refining.

At this point, we can think through the implementation of some of these ideas in order to see how they might play out (the last thing you want to do is solve one problem while creating three more). For each possible direction, what steps would be required to put it into action? What are the strengths or potential upsides of each idea? What are the possible challenges or unintended consequences of implementing each approach? This process can be done live with everyone in a meeting or on your own with other key decision-makers (after which the results would be transparently relayed back to the stakeholders).

While going through this evaluation process, there may well be a natural narrowing down of ideas—leaving you with a clear sense of your best options.

Step 4: Finalize Decisions

Now, we've landed on some final options, each with potential upsides that outweigh the potential downsides. If the decision you are making allows for more collaboration from here, take these vetted ideas and focus-group them with stakeholders from areas of the organization that would be impacted by the decision. Make sure to seek out diverse perspectives from within these areas. You might even get perspectives from other departments or teams that will not be affected by the decision and, therefore, may not have been involved in the decision-making process thus far.

During the finalization process, lay out clearly and transparently how each potential direction would be implemented, how you'll measure its success, what accountability would look like for each scenario, and the pros and cons of each potential decision. Make sure that you set realistic expectations upfront. You don't need to incorporate all feedback, but make sure to be flexible where possible, as this will increase buy-in and ownership over the implementation of your decisions. Remember, people don't always need to get their way to feel empowered at work—they simply need to feel heard and that their ideas are actually considered.

Step 5: Communicate Decisions Transparently

After you gather feedback from stakeholders who would be impacted by the decision, be sure to follow up with all who were involved in the decision-making process, regardless of whether or not you incorporated their feedback. Let your team know that you heard their feedback and had to weigh many factors in reaching your decision. Explain as appropriately as you can how you came to the final decision, what options and ideas you considered, and why you believe the current direction has the most upside and the least potential downside.

As a Peaceful Leader, you are required to make countless decisions every day. Some may be small, and others may impact certain individuals or the entire organization in significant ways. Not all decisions require a formal process to be inclusive. But the next time you have to make a decision, think about how to incorporate the key principles and steps outlined in this section. Empowering your team to take ownership over the direction and success of the organization through inclusive decision-making is critical for cultivating a peaceful and engaged workplace culture.

Promoting Accountability

In the context of this book, **accountability** refers to a leader's ability to create clear and realistic expectations for their employees and to *empower* them to follow through and meet those expectations. Understanding how to appropriately hold people accountable is critical for Peaceful Leaders. If, for example, a leader is punitive or reactive when holding people accountable, they risk diminishing the trust and safety within their team because employees become afraid to fail or make mistakes. However, if a leader doesn't hold people accountable at all, they send the message that expectations don't matter, which can alienate, confuse, or demotivate the team members who *are* meeting expectations and ultimately devalue any expectations you set in the future. Either of these trajectories ultimately leads to conflict.

Consequently, it's imperative you find a way to hold people accountable for their actions, behaviors, and work product while also empowering them to take ownership and pride over their role in the organization. What follows is a five-step process for weaving accountability into the fabric of your team's culture. If implemented properly, it will be much easier for you to hold employees responsible for meeting expectations without coming across as vindictive, biased, or punitive.

Step 1: Establish Agreed-Upon Expectations

The importance of setting expectations may be obvious. What can be less obvious is the importance of setting *mutually agreed-upon expectations.* Certainly, these may still be *your* expectations about how people ought to behave, communicate, or perform. But if others don't agree with the expectations in the first place, they won't feel empowered to take ownership of meeting them. So, when you want to see specific behaviors, communications, or work products from your team, be sure to approach the expectation-setting process as a more inclusive dialogue to determine whether employees agree with and see the value in your expectations. This will help you reinforce expectations in the future because you can refer back to agreements that they themselves made rather than to expectations you unilaterally imposed.

Step 2: Create Specific and Clear Goals

Once people know what they're accountable for, it's important to give them a clear explanation of what successfully meeting expectations looks like. In other words, whereas expectations may be broadly defined, goals are specific and measurable markers of meeting those broad expectations. If you have an agreed-upon expectation for timely workplace communication, for example, you'd want to quantify what timeliness means. Should people respond within two hours? Four hours? Within the same day?

When it comes to setting goals for a work project, it's best to get specific on what exactly will be done, when, and by whom. Who owns what parts of the project, what deliverables are expected, and when exactly are they to be delivered? In addition, try to incorporate your criteria for success so everyone knows exactly how their product or deliverable will be evaluated. Don't assume that others know exactly what is expected just because you do—explicitly state and gain agreement over the goals, writing them down for everyone to reference in the future.

Ultimately, it's hard to hold people accountable for achieving goals in an empowering way when there's confusion about what said goals are. The clearer and more specific you can get, the less room there will be for misinterpretation.

Step 3: Check in Regularly

Once you create specific and clear goals, make sure to set an agreed-upon schedule for checking in on your team's progress. With work projects or in situations where you're helping a team member make changes in their communication or behavior, it's good to check in regularly just to make sure things are on track. This creates a space for you to give and receive feedback, whether positive or constructive, and thus to get ahead of any issues; it also allows you to offer assistance or, if necessary, modify agreed-upon expectations to promote empowerment and sustainable success.

In general, after setting agreed-upon expectations regarding communication, norms, policies, or procedures, it is still a good practice to revisit and review these items on at least an annual basis to update and refine them. This will help keep goals and standards current while also serving as a reminder as to what the expectations are.

Step 4: Empower Through Challenges

After setting expectations clearly with the team, some challenges in meeting those expectations are bound to arise. When these challenges do arise, do your best to address them in a timely manner. Lest they grow larger, don't sit back and hope the challenges will just go away on their own; waiting to tackle them can reduce accountability and subsequently hamper employee trust.

When you notice people having difficulty meeting expectations, you don't want to assert your power by dictating solutions, calling team members out in public, or trying to motivate through fear. Instead, aim to empower. Ask questions to better understand what's working, what isn't, and how you can work together to overcome obstacles. As a Peaceful Leader, you should strive to be an ally who offers support rather than a dictator who poses a threat. (If the situation calls for a difficult conversation with your employees, make sure to review the skills outlined in Chapter 8.)

Step 5: Celebrate Successes

When your team makes progress, meets or exceeds their expectations, and achieves their goals, celebrate those successes with them. That doesn't mean you have to have a company party every time someone meets expectations. Simple acknowledgments honoring their hard work and highlighting their impact can motivate people to hold themselves accountable to agreed-upon expectations in the future. Equally important, these celebrations make accountability and accomplishments fun, not distressing.

Self-Accountability

As a Peaceful Leader, you should hold yourself accountable as much as or more than everyone else on your team. The success of your team starts and stops with you, which means that you share in both their successes and missteps. When a team member fails to meet expectations, it is, in part, a reflection of your ability to set clear goals or appropriately foster accountability. If you simply blame others or excuse your own behavior or communication, you set the tone for what is acceptable in your workplace. At the end of the day, your role is to ensure your team has the resources, skills, and support to be successful; for your team to buy into a culture of Radical Ownership and accountability, you need to lead by example.

So, as you think about how to incorporate accountability practices into the culture of your organization and team, start with how you can hold yourself accountable: What can you do better moving forward? How can you better support your team and empower them to take ownership of their actions and the team's success?

The skills you learned in this chapter are critical for fostering a workplace culture where your team members feel like they are included in decisions that impact them, that they have some control over their environment, and that they're empowered to excel in their work and truly meet their goals.

Case Narrative: Empowerment

As Connor and Renee worked towards building out their future-focused agreement, Connor remained mindful and considerate of the hierarchy that existed, ensuring that Renee felt heard, aware of his intentions, and cognizant of the accountability within the team. Connor didn't want the impromptu team meetings to send the wrong message to Renee or anyone else. That's why part of their agreement was to ensure better dissemination of information, schedule regular team meetings, and have a plan for bringing in HR to address issues before they escalate.

Through participating in this Peacemaking process, both Connor and Renee learned to better give and receive feedback, focus on strengths rather than weaknesses, and learn to slow down and respond to situations rather than react impulsively. The power dynamic was important for Connor to consider in all his interactions with Renee and other team members. He would need to become more mindful of his words and actions, which would help his relationships at work and, ultimately, his career. Regardless of the power dynamic, however, both individuals learned they could practice leadership skills, which were useful not just at work but in all walks of life.

Connor soon went on to complete our Peaceful Leaders Academy to further enhance his ability to foster psychological safety, employee trust, and inclusion in his warehouse. Renee, too, gained the empowerment and motivation she needed to improve her leadership skills as she went on to become a Senior IT Systems Analyst.

It's not without consistent practice that these skills become a more natural response to challenging situations. Being a Peaceful Leader requires more than a certification program. It requires a commitment to lifelong learning, illustrated through consistent practice and embodiment of patience, engagement, appreciation, curiosity, and empowerment.

STRATEGY SESSION

Okay, let's see how you could empower your team. See if you can finish the following sentences.

I would be a more empowering leader if I......

If I did that, I would be more effective as a leader because......

A challenge for me to grow in this area is.....

To overcome this challenge, I can......

My first step to being a more empowering leader is......

Conclusion

According to the U.S. Equal Employment Opportunity Commission (EEOC),[43] more than 60,000 employment-related lawsuits were filed in 2022, resulting in more than $30 million in legal awards granted by federal courts. This does not include hundreds of millions of dollars awarded to plaintiffs each year in state and local civil courts. Some of these cases may have been unavoidable, no matter the effectiveness of company leadership. Inevitably, however, many of these cases were due to supervisors being unable and/or unwilling to properly address conflicts before they spiraled out of control. In fact, many of these conflicts could have likely been resolved long before adjudication if the plaintiffs simply felt listened to and cared for by their leaders.

At the end of the day, we're all just human beings. Some of us have fancy titles, while others are entry-level workers.

---

[43] EEOC. (2022). *Charge Statistics (Charges filed with EEOC) FY 1997 Through FY 2021*. Retrieved from: https://www.eeoc.gov/statistics/charge-statistics-charges-filed-eeoc-fy-1997-through-fy-2021

Some of us work in offices, while others work in the field or out on the factory floor. Some of us work 9 to 5, while others take the night shift. No matter what we do for work, or where or how we do it, we all share a very basic, primitive set of psychological needs—to feel secure, to feel respected, to know we are accepted by our groups, and to have some control over our lives. When these needs are unfulfilled by any cultural system—be it a workplace or a society—conflict is what follows. When these needs are satisfied, peace is the natural result.

After reading this material, we hope you feel significantly more confident handling challenging situations as they arise and, ultimately, satisfying the fundamental needs of your team. By modeling and embodying patience, engagement, appreciation, curiosity, and empowerment, you set the tone for a workplace that fosters psychological safety, employee trust, and inclusive practices.

For more in-depth training and coaching in these skills through the framework of Peaceful Leadership or to become a *Certified Peaceful Leader*™, visit us at www.PeacefulLeadersAcademy.com.

About the Authors

Jeremy Pollack, Ph.D.

Jeremy is a social-organizational psychologist and a leader in the field of workplace conflict resolution and peacebuilding. He is the Founder of Pollack Peacebuilding Systems, a nationwide workplace conflict resolution consulting firm. He is also co-founder and chairman of the Peaceful Leadership Institute, a 501c3 non-profit dedicated to promoting the model and theory of Peaceful Leadership, as well as co-founder and Chairman of the Association for Conflict Resolution, Florida, a non-profit aimed at supporting the practice and field of conflict resolution in the state of Florida.

Jeremy is a coach, trainer, mediator, and author. He coaches and trains executives and employees at a variety of levels and industries, from Fortune 100 companies to major non-profits. Jeremy has mediated conflicts between business partners, co-executives, and coworkers at all levels of organizations, aiming as often as possible to transform relationships and create Win-Win resolutions for all parties involved.

Jeremy has been a regular contributor on the topics of leadership and organizational conflict management to publications such as Forbes.com, Fast Company, Industry Week, and many more. He is also the author of the *The Conflict Resolution Playbook: Practical Communication Skills for Preventing, Managing, and Resolving, Conflict.*

Jeremy holds a Ph.D. in Psychology, a Master's degree in Negotiation, Conflict Resolution, and Peacebuilding (NCRP), and a Master's degree in Evolutionary Anthropology. He is also a Certified Organizational Development Coach (CODC™), a Certified Clinical Trauma Specialist - Individual (CCST-I™), a Certified Workplace Mindfulness Facilitator (CWMF™), and an Associate Certified Coach (ACC) under the International Coaching Federation. He formerly served as a research fellow at Stanford University's Center for International Conflict & Negotiation, where he led research projects in social psychology and conflict resolution, and prior to that as a research associate at UCLA's Center for Behavior, Evolution, and Culture. Currently, he is a faculty member in the psychology department at Arizona College of Nursing.

Luke Wiesner, M.S.

In 2012, Luke's research on cyberbullying intervention strategies at Western Washington University ignited a passion for facilitating constructive and compassionate communication during conflicts. This pivotal experience set the stage for his career as a Conflict Resolution Professional, where he has collaborated with hundreds of organizations across the United States, Canada, and Europe, spanning diverse industries such as government, education, healthcare, hospitality, technology, manufacturing, and finance.

As an NLP and ICF Professional Certified Coach and Mediator with a Master's of Science degree in Conflict Resolution and Organizational Leadership from Creighton University, Luke's work focuses on creating breakthrough realizations and transformative discoveries for his clients. By dedicating over 2500 direct service hours to providing mediation, coaching, training, and facilitation, he brings a process-oriented approach and a curiosity to uncover the underlying interests, needs, and goals to surface in honest and direct dialogue about challenges disrupting organizational performance and employee well-being. Luke identifies successful outcomes when his clients can verbalize specific evidence of sustained organizational growth and relationship transformation.

Luke is a co-founder of Peaceful Leadership and collaborates closely with his colleagues, Jeremy Pollack and Sara Jeckovich. Together, they are dedicated to creating peaceful and conflict-resilient workplace cultures. Their collective efforts aim to redefine how individuals and organizations navigate conflicts, communication, and professional relationships.

Sara Jeckovich, M.A.

Sara works with individuals and teams on building their effective communication and conflict management skills. As a Peacebuilder and Program Director with Pollack Peacebuilding Systems, Sara guides her clients through Training, Coaching, Mediation and Facilitation services. Her experiences working in trauma-informed care and with multicultural groups are drivers of her work. From Case Management and Client Services to Coaching and Facilitating group dynamics, Sara's experience brings structure and heart to her Peacebuilding work. She has developed training curricula for international NGOs working with refugees in resettlement, managed and supported teams within nonprofit organizations, as well as assisted in the creation of standardized practices for public and private sector organizations.

Working as a Peacebuilder with Pollack Peacebuilding Systems, Sara has coached and facilitated individuals and teams from various industries, helping to enhance their abilities to communicate effectively with one another through challenging times, while increasing efficiency, productivity, and overall well-being. Sara holds a Master of Arts degree in Peacebuilding and Conflict Transformation from the School for International Training Graduate Institute, and sees leadership as an *attribute* rather than a *title*.

www.ingramcontent.com/pod-product-compliance
Lightning Source LLC
Chambersburg PA
CBHW032054020426
42335CB00011B/333